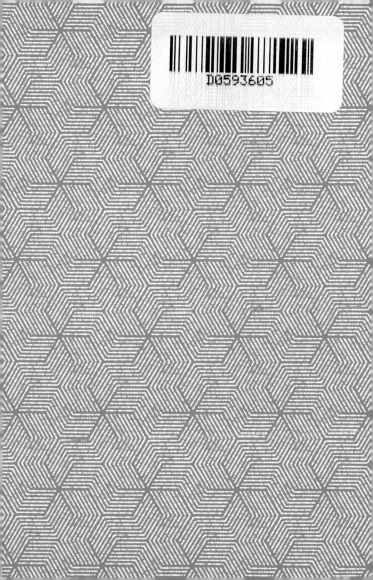

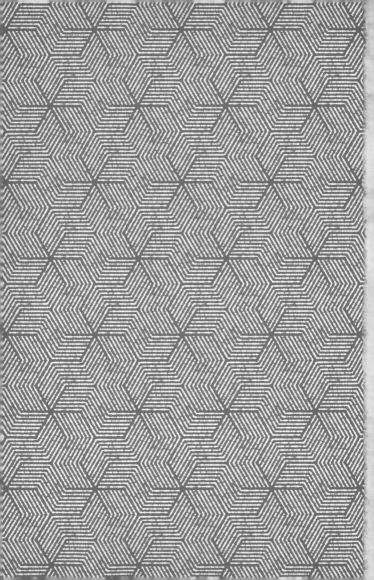

Inspirations for a Slower, Simpler
& More Soulful Life

sand
between
your
toes

by Anna Kettle

Tyndale House Publishers
Carol Stream, Illinois

**LIVING
EXPRESSIONS**
COLLECTION

Living Expressions invites you to explore
God's Word in a way that is refreshing to
the spirit and restorative to the soul.

Visit Tyndale online at tyndale.com.

TYNDALE, Tyndale's quill logo, *Living Expressions*, and the Living Expressions
logo are registered trademarks of Tyndale House Ministries.

*Sand Between Your Toes: Inspirations for a Slower, Simpler, and More
Soulful Life*

Designed by Libby Dykstra

For information about special discounts for bulk purchases, please contact
Tyndale House Publishers at csresponse@tyndale.com, or call 1-800-323-9400.

ISBN 978-1-4964-4388-5

Printed in China

26	25	24	23	22	21	20
7	6	5	4	3	2	1

Have you never heard?
Have you never understood?
The LORD is the everlasting God,
the Creator of all the earth.
He never grows weak or weary.
No one can measure the depths
of his understanding.

He gives power to the weak
and strength to the powerless.

ISAIAH 40:28-29

Anchored in Love

*Surely your goodness and unfailing love
will pursue me all the days of my life.*

PSALM 23:6

I love this verse because it's such a sure promise these days when certainty doesn't seem like a very common currency.

We live in times of political, social, and economic instability, not to mention rapid technological change. All those factors can leave us longing for some constancy in our lives.

Some people search for that sense of stability by believing that we need to go back to the good old days. Others simply try to control their present reality in equally unhealthy ways.

But the truth is that we can't go back and recreate what has already been; we can only go forward into our future. The good news is we can do it with hopeful hearts that are laid wide open to God's love.

His goodness and unfailing love are undisputed certainties. They have remained unchanged throughout the ages, truly standing the test of time. And they aren't hidden away or hard to find either.

The Bible says that his goodness and love are actively pursuing us; pursuing us in the same way that a man pursues a woman or a treasure hunter chases clues—proactively, passionately, and urgently. What an incredible thought!

I desperately want a life that is overflowing with God's goodness and love, don't you? When we commit ourselves to him, he promises to give us just that.

∾ Pause and Sift ∾

How confident are you of God's goodness and love? Spend a few minutes reflecting on some of the different ways you've experienced him pursuing you throughout your life.

Lord, today I am opening my heart afresh to experiencing your goodness and your love. Please fill me to overflowing so they can impact every aspect of my life.

Still Yourself

Be still, and know that I am God!

PSALM 46:10

Being still is so countercultural in a world that is always moving, isn't it? And it's also really hard to do!

I grew up in a Christian family and was taught from a young age the importance of regularly setting aside time to spend with God. But even now, at forty, I struggle with being still before him.

Because I'm such a doer, "being still" has always sounded, well . . . a little bit boring to me. But these days, I find myself craving more stillness.

I'm a full-time working mom with a busy schedule. I juggle the responsibilities of parent-hood and running a household alongside the pressures of a career, and I try to keep some semblance of a social life. Sometimes the expectations of modern life can feel relentless, can't they?

What about you? Are you frequently exhausted

and longing to slow down, yet discovering that it's difficult to create any margin for rest in your life? Do you often find yourself mentally harassed by all the things that need to be checked off while struggling to relax, feeling that you should be doing something more productive?

I love today's verse because it reminds me that we're not human robots designed for ever-greater levels of efficiency; we're human beings created to be in relationship with our Maker and called to live in his love.

So let's connect with God in stillness today, remembering who he is.

∾ Pause and Sift ∾

Take a few moments to sit quietly in God's presence. Turn off your phone and push aside all other distractions. Simply focus on who he is and let that truth begin to change your perspective.

Lord, I know that I often move through life at a pace that isn't good for my soul. Help me learn how to still myself before you.

Ask for Help

He gives grace generously.

JAMES 4:6

Are you stretched to the limit, pulled in too many directions, and overwhelmed by a myriad of tasks? Do you frequently find yourself struggling to slow down for fear of dropping the ball?

Me too. And yet if I'm honest, more often than not I choose to keep relying on my own strength rather than asking for the help that I need. Does that sound familiar?

This verse assures us that we don't need to run ourselves ragged and work ourselves to the bone, because God freely and generously offers us his grace.

Grace means not having to do all things and know all things and be all things, all the time, and yet still knowing that you are held in his love.

All you need to do to receive this gift of grace is to humbly ask for it. Grace doesn't run out—it isn't rationed and is never in short supply. You can't use up your quota for the day. There is always more available!

Even when God gives an outrageously generous amount to someone else, it doesn't hamper his ability to abundantly give grace to you too. His grace reserves are infinite. There is more than enough to go around.

So ask him for his grace today. Take as much as you need. And then take some extra, just in case.

∾ Pause and Sift ∾

Try praying on the go throughout your day. Invite God into each of your full-on, crazy moments, even as they're happening, and simply ask him to give you his grace.

Lord, I'm sorry for the times when I insist on relying solely on my own strength rather than humbling myself and asking for your grace. I need it, moment by moment and day by day.

Practice Self-Care

*Don't you realize that your body
is the temple of the Holy Spirit, who lives
in you and was given to you by God?*

1 CORINTHIANS 6:19

What do you think of when you hear the word
self-care? Does it seem like a luxury, an indul-
gence, or just something that's reserved for
people with plenty of money and spare time?

Incredibly, there's an $11 billion self-care
industry in the United States today, dedicated
to promoting practices such as eating better,
being active, sleeping well, reducing stress, and
prioritizing "me time."

But the idea of practicing good self-care is
really nothing new. It's age-old wisdom that's
encouraged in the Bible too.

As important as it is to maintain our spiritual
health, today's verse reminds us that our bodies
and minds are just as important.

What we put into our bodies matters. We need

to eat good, nourishing food that gives us energy and strength.

Regular exercise matters too. We need to get on our feet and be active to help reduce the risk of developing health problems.

But that's not all. What we *think* also matters. We need to fill our minds with thoughts that are good, pure, and true.

Caring for every part of ourselves is a spiritual matter because as followers of Jesus, each one of us is a temple of the Holy Spirit. We have been bought at a very high price—the life of God's only Son. Do you know how valuable that makes each one of us?

∿ Pause and Sift ∿

Make one small lifestyle change today that supports better self-care. Share your goal with someone you trust and ask that person to keep you accountable.

Lord, I choose to honor my body, mind, and spirit today by practicing good self-care, remembering how much my life cost you and how much you value me.

Say No

Yes, my soul, find rest in God;
my hope comes from him.

PSALM 62:5, NIV

Our culture is obsessed with *more*: more work, more money, more achievements, more success, more influence, more stuff.

More can also sound like the most spiritual or selfless option, can't it? More commitment, more activity, more self-sacrifice, more service.

But sometimes less is more. Less rushing around, less cramming things in, less spreading yourself too thin, and less pushing yourself so hard can be much more beneficial.

In fact, sometimes saying no is the single most spiritual thing we can do. Too often when we take on more, we are actually people-pleasing—trying to impress others rather than accomplishing what God wants us to do.

It can be so easy to slip into believing that saying yes is always the better option, because *yes* is the word that makes things happen. If we don't do it, who will?

Often we end up putting the needs of everyone else—our families and friends—before our own. But saying no when you already feel overstretched and overloaded in order to prioritize the health of your own soul is not selfish; it's necessary. And it's also the right thing to do, both for you and for those around you.

You simply can't give what you don't have, and you can't care for others well if you don't care for yourself.

Turn down a project. Drop some commitments. Put your hope in God, not in how much you can do, and discover deeper rest for your soul.

∿ Pause and Sift ∿

Practice saying no to a few of the things you have always said yes to. Let some of the less important stuff slide.

Lord, I tend to choose more things instead of the right things. Would you give me greater clarity about when to say yes and when to say no?

11

Use the Delays

*Endurance develops strength of character,
and character strengthens our confident
hope of salvation. And this hope will
not lead to disappointment.*

ROMANS 5:4-5

I was recently standing in a checkout line at the store when my phone battery died. I was irritated. I couldn't scroll, email, text, or multitask. There was nothing for me to do except put the phone away and accept a few minutes of dead time.

Getting frustrated with short periods of waiting is kind of irrational since things don't happen any faster when we get stressed out. In fact, our impatience rarely changes anything; it only makes the waiting harder.

Have I really become someone who can't just relax and do nothing for a few minutes without growing incomprehensibly bored? Well, it turns out I'm not alone. Google has found that 53 percent of us will abandon a mobile page if it takes longer than three seconds to load. That's how low our threshold for waiting has become!

But what if we learned to see its value? I think there have been important lessons in all the waiting I've ever done, whether the more mundane kind, which reminds me to be more present, or the longer-term kind, such as hoping for a breakthrough.

Today's verse is a good reminder that waiting rewards us with patience, perseverance, and character. Maybe God is more interested in who we are becoming as we wait than he is in our perceived inconvenience.

∼ Pause and Sift ∼

Force yourself to wait today. Deliberately pick the longest checkout line in the store or take the heaviest traffic route. Use the delays to spend time with God and even pray for those who are waiting with you.

Lord, you know waiting is difficult for me
and that I struggle with being patient.
Would you teach me how to wait well
throughout every delay?

Leave Regret Behind

Anyone who belongs to Christ has become a new person. The old life is gone; a new life has begun!

2 CORINTHIANS 5:17

Regret. We all know how it feels. Maybe something didn't happen the way that you wanted it to. Perhaps you did something you wish you could undo or said something you would rather take back.

When we fail to deal with regret, it can leave us feeling trapped in guilt or shame, and that's a heavy burden to keep carrying around.

The solution? Deal with things quickly and make amends if necessary, but then let yourself off the hook. After all, regret is often about not being able to forgive yourself.

We can't undo the past, but as followers of Jesus, we are offered a fresh start, a slate wiped clean of sin. The Bible says that when we receive Jesus as our Savior, we become new people.

We're no longer under the obligation to do what our old, sinful natures try to convince us to do. Instead, we can choose to live in step with God's indwelling Spirit, who has pronounced us clean and forgiven. Who are we to argue by not forgiving ourselves?

Regret is focused on the past. Worry is occupying yourself with the future. But the present is here within your grasp, and you get to choose a life marked by God's grace.

∾ Pause and Sift ∾

Spend some time considering your identity in Christ. Choose a relevant verse to memorize, and begin each day saying it out loud to yourself.

Lord, thank you for your grace that frees me from regret. Help me to live in the truth that the past has passed, but the present is full of new promise because I am your child—forgiven, loved, and free.

"Maybe Now" Moments

You will show me the way of life,
granting me the joy of your presence.

PSALM 16:11

What is that "one thing" you want to happen right now? Perhaps it's getting a promotion or hitting that magic number on your scale; maybe it's getting married or buying your dream house.

We've probably all had those "maybe now" moments in life, when we've told ourselves "Maybe now that this has happened . . . I'll feel content" or "If only that would happen . . . maybe then my life would be complete."

When I was in my twenties, I believed the prerequisite for happiness was being married, then achieving a dream career, creating the perfect home, and having several children.

Hoping for good things isn't bad as long as they don't become greater than our desire for the One who gives them.

We live in a consumer culture that is constantly trying to persuade us that we need something more in order to be happy. But if we think that we'll ever really find joy through buying more stuff, achieving more success, chasing a certain dream, or even falling in love, we will only burn ourselves out in the process of our pursuit.

And even if we do eventually end up getting our "maybe now" moment, chances are that it will probably still leave us dissatisfied. Yes, it can add to our joy, but nothing in this world can complete us or even make our joy complete. Temporary experiences were never meant to.

True joy is found only in God and we've had access to his presence all along.

∾ Pause and Sift ∾

How do you connect with God best? Through music, creative projects, time outdoors, or something else? Set aside some personal time this week and rediscover the joy of his presence.

Lord, today I am simply choosing to spend time in your presence because I know it's the only way to truly satisfy my soul.

ꝰGuard Your Heart

Guard your heart above all else,
for it determines the course of your life.

PROVERBS 4:23

Has this ever happened to you? You got frustrated or wound up about something trivial and then thought afterward, *What is wrong with me?*

Maybe you lost your patience with your spouse or unfairly shouted at your kids and a moment later wished you hadn't. If I'm honest, I overreact more than I'd care to admit.

I wonder whether some of those emotional human outbursts come from never really creating the time and space to process life as it happens or to properly deal with life's impact on our hearts.

Today's verse affirms that what's inside our hearts can stay hidden for a time, but sooner or later it will end up seeping into our words and influencing our actions. And what's more, these pent-up emotions will probably spill out at the wrong time or onto the wrong person, especially when we feel stressed.

So it's really worth taking some time out for regular self-reflection and proactively processing our emotions.

Guarding your heart means being brave enough to deal with any hurts, disappointments, or offenses as they happen instead of just shelving things until a later date, which often never comes.

Here's my advice: Don't neglect or put off until tomorrow those things you could deal with today. The shape that your heart is in really does determine how healthy every part of your life will be.

∿ Pause and Sift ∿

Quickly check your emotional pulse at the end of your day. Ask God to show you any emotional baggage you might need to deal with. If you find this helpful, make it a regular practice.

Lord, give me greater awareness about the true state of my heart. Help me to guard it well so that the course of my life honors you.

Day by Day

Give us today the food we need.

MATTHEW 6:11

It's often human nature to want to hoard, to save up, and to keep a little extra on the side—just in case!

But God has always been looking for a people who will depend on him to meet their needs. Just look at how he supplied food for the Israelites every morning when they were wandering through the desert, teaching them not to store it up but to trust in his fresh provision each day.

Have you ever been financially stretched? It can be one of the most anxiety-inducing situations we will experience. My husband and I faced a period with uncomfortably small margins in our finances just after our son was born. My salary was lower during my maternity leave, and my husband was in the process of setting up his own business.

Just like the Israelites, we suddenly found ourselves forced to depend on God's provision because after paying all the bills with each paycheck, we didn't have any surplus left over. We learned to live day by day and week by week, trusting God to fill any gaps.

I didn't enjoy feeling so out of control, but that discomfort pushed us to trust God in deeper ways. And do you know what? As we asked him to provide, we found there was always just enough.

It can be difficult looking to God to meet our needs, whether they're financial, practical, emotional, or spiritual. But as we trust him day by day, he promises to provide for us each day as well.

∾ Pause and Sift ∾

Do you need extra energy, grace, peace, patience, strength, or finances? Ask God to supply enough for today.

Lord, I'm sorry that I tend to be independent and self-sufficient. Help me to look to you as my provider, rather than relying only on what I can earn for myself.

Turn Down the Noise

Let all that I am wait quietly before God,
for my hope is in him.

PSALM 62:5

Do you ever feel overwhelmed by the endless
to-do list in your head?

It nags at you with housework, school pickups,
grocery shopping, fitness classes, work commitments, church obligations, social events, things to
follow up on from yesterday, and things to orga-
nize for tomorrow.

If that weren't enough, an endless stream
of information is constantly vying for your
attention—texts, tweets, posts, discussions, direct
messages, conversation threads, emails, phone
calls, app alerts, news articles, advertisements,
podcasts, playlists, TV shows, and more. The
continuous noise we allow into our lives can be
deafening.

Are you on Facebook? Each day more than
300 million photos get uploaded, and each minute 510,000 comments are posted and 293,000

statuses are updated. Do you use Twitter? An incredible 500 million new tweets are posted every single day!

The digital age has created a world where true silence is becoming harder to find and tuning in to what God is saying is more difficult.

Maybe there's a direct correlation between the amount of noise we allow into our lives and our inability to hear God's voice as clearly or as often as we would like to. Are you providing enough silence in your day for a personal connection?

∽ Pause and Sift ∾

Be silent for ten minutes before God today—no words and no agenda. Just listen and create space for his presence. If your mind drifts off, remember today's verse and bring your focus back.

Lord, I recognize that there's often too much noise in my life. Help me to be more deliberate about turning it all down on a regular basis so that your voice might become louder in my life.

Writing in Pencil

We can make our plans,
but the Lord determines our steps.

PROVERBS 16:9

Most of us like to believe we're in control of our lives—until something unexpected happens and turns things upside down.

You have plans—then suddenly God interrupts them. You start a new business, but it doesn't take off. You're buying a house, but the sale falls through. You begin a new project, but ill health gets in the way.

Sometimes what seems like an irritating change can actually be a kindness. Perhaps God is intervening to help prevent us from making a huge mistake, or because our plans have veered off course from his.

At other times, it's not at all clear why he allows our lives to be disrupted. All we know is that it's inconvenient, unsettling, and often painful. Sometimes it involves letting go or saying goodbye to people or places we love.

It can be emotionally grueling when things don't work out quite as we'd hoped. But whenever I find myself facing the unexpected or struggling to wait for God's plan to unfold, it helps me to remember that only he knows where the next chapter of my story will lead.

He is the author of my life; he knows the beginning and the end, and I can trust him with the details.

Our best-laid plans are all good, just as long as we hold them lightly, write them in pencil, and remain open to God's unexpected edits and rewrites.

∽ **Pause and Sift** ∽

Are you frustrated with how your plans are unfolding?
Try letting go of your own time line and expectations
and being ready and willing to go with God's plans.

Lord, I'm sorry that I often try to write my own
narrative rather than trusting in yours for me.
Today I am making tentative plans, knowing
that they are subject to change
according to your purpose.

An Open Invitation

*Look! I stand at the door and knock. If you hear
my voice and open the door, I will come in, and
we will share a meal together as friends.*

REVELATION 3:20

Today's verse is often interpreted as a description
of the moment before someone first becomes a
Christian. Jesus is knocking at the door of our
hearts, waiting for us to ask him in.

While this may be true, I wonder if it misses
part of the meaning. Is opening the door to Jesus
really meant to be only a once-in-a-lifetime act?
Does he ever really stop knocking at the door to
our hearts?

I believe he wants to be invited into our
lives every day. He wants to come in to talk and
spend time with us. That's how you build any
relationship.

Often we speak about wanting to draw closer
to God, but maybe he is already very close and is
just waiting for the invitation to enter more deeply
into our lives. Could it be we're so busy that we

fail to hear his knock or make the time to welcome him?

Jesus won't ram the door and force his way in. Instead he simply stands outside and waits, like any neighbor or good friend would.

I don't know about you, but I don't want to leave Jesus out in the cold. I want to invite him to take residence in my life every single day.

∾ Pause and Sift ∾

When you sit down to eat today, invite Jesus to be a guest at your table. Say a prayer, read Scripture, or light a candle to help you be aware of his presence.

Lord, I invite you to make my heart your home today and every day. There is nothing more important than sharing my life with you.

Plan to Rest

God blessed the seventh day and declared it holy,
because it was the day when he rested from all his work.

GENESIS 2:3

How is it possible that I've almost reached the
halfway point in my life but still have never really
learned the art of resting well?

Perhaps a lot of the exhaustion I feel is caused
by my inability to switch off, tune out, unplug, and
get off-line.

Too often I find myself feeling drained at
the end of the day, crashing in front of the TV,
aimlessly scrolling through Facebook posts, or
googling websites to buy things I don't need.
Although those moments on the sofa might seem
physically relaxing, I am not giving myself what
I actually need: mental downtime and rest for
my soul.

I doubt I'm alone in feeling this way.

Maybe true rest is less about physically stopping and more about resting the mind; maybe it's

less about doing nothing and more about doing something different instead.

Of course, our need to regularly rest from work is not a news flash for our Creator! The concept of "Sabbath"—taking one day in seven to step away from the schedule, the to-do list, and the routine—was his idea, after all.

And if God himself has been modeling rest to us ever since the Creation story in Genesis, then maybe it's something we should consider paying a little more attention to.

∿ Pause and Sift ∿

Take a short inventory: Are you resting enough? Is it quality rest? Do you regularly practice stepping away from your routine? Or do you need to schedule some rest?

Lord, teach me how to adopt the idea of
Sabbath more. Help me to better pace myself
and develop regular rhythms of rest in my life,
just as you have always intended for me.

Live Fully

I have come that they may have life, and have it to the full.

JOHN 10:10, NIV

As Christians we're promised life to the full, but what does that really mean? Is every day meant to feel like a superturbocharged, adrenaline-pumping Pepsi Max or Red Bull moment? Personally, I don't think so.

We live in a world that's obsessed with the "big Hollywood" moment—that dramatic season finale, that rags-to-riches story, that romantic first kiss when two people fall in love, that life-changing scene when an ordinary kid is trans-formed into a pop superstar.

I wonder how often this "big moment" kind of thinking can seep into our theology and our churches too. For instance, how many songs and sermons have you heard about stepping into your own history-making, world-changing calling?

When we feed on a constant media diet of sensationalized entertainment, is it all that surprising to find that so many of us feel our lives are just a bit too boring and ordinary?

Slowly I'm coming to the realization that most of life doesn't happen as high-octane, straight-out-of-a-movie-script scenes. It happens in millions of small details and everyday moments.

When Jesus said he came to give us life to the full, surely he meant for us to experience it in our present-day realities and not in some distant daydreams.

Maybe fullness of life is what's already unfolding right in front of us, in each of these ordinary spaces in our lives, shared with an extraordinary God.

∾ Pause and Sift ∾

Seek beauty in your everyday moments. Try to slow down and savor the ordinary things, and find fresh wonder even in the mundane. You'll be surprised at what you discover.

Lord, my life is a gift from you that I get to open every day. Help me to remember that there's nothing more exciting or more sacred than this "ordinary" life I get to share with you.

Find Freedom

*"Lord, how often should I forgive someone who
sins against me? Seven times?" "No, not seven
times," Jesus replied, "but seventy times seven!"*

MATTHEW 18:21-22

Forgiveness is rarely a onetime act. But exactly
how often do we have to keep forgiving someone
when they keep hurting us or treating us badly?

When Peter posed this question to Jesus, it's
possible he was thinking of Jesus' words in Luke
17:3-4: "If another believer sins, rebuke that person; then if there is repentance, forgive. Even if
that person wrongs you seven times a day and
each time turns again and asks forgiveness, you
must forgive."

But in today's passage, Jesus goes even further.
"Don't keep count. Forgive someone as many
times as you need to until you are freed from
lingering resentment."

At first, offering forgiveness can feel unfair
because it seems like we're saying that whatever
happened didn't matter and that we don't deserve

justice. But forgiveness invites us to exchange our anger, hurt, and bitterness for God's peace, healing, and freedom.

If you are harboring a grudge in your heart, why not ask God to take up the matter instead?

It isn't about letting someone else off the hook; it's about trusting God to deal with the other person. And much more than that, it's about allowing him to free you from the emotional hold he or she still has over you.

Forgiveness is certainly not easy, and it's not a guaranteed fix for a broken relationship. God never promised that it would be. But it's always worth it for the experience of living free.

∾ Pause and Sift ∾

Is there anyone you need to forgive? Make that choice today, and keep on making it as many times as it takes to become fully free.

Lord, help me to forgive others freely and trust you to handle the situation rather than taking matters into my own hands.

Resist Being Overwhelmed

Be strong and courageous, and do the work.
Don't be afraid or discouraged, for the LORD God,
my God, is with you. He will not fail you or forsake you.

1 CHRONICLES 28:20

Have you ever felt overwhelmed by the size of
a task in front of you or by the sheer weight of
responsibility?

I'm guessing every new parent recalls the
moment they were told they could take their baby
home. I will never forget the day that my husband, Andy, and I left the hospital with our son.
It was totally nerve-racking. Instead of feeling
delighted, we just wanted to say, "Are you sure?
We're not qualified for this! We don't know what
we're doing!" I don't think Andy has ever driven
anywhere so slowly!

Today's verse recounts King David's encouraging words to his son Solomon, who was charged
to build God's Temple. Maybe Solomon had

fears about this daunting assignment. Maybe he believed it was too big to handle.

You weren't asked to build the Temple, but maybe you're working on a challenging project that leaves you feeling out of your depth. Perhaps you're pioneering a new ministry, building a new business, or writing your first book.

If God has called you to this work, he will strengthen you to complete it. He promises never to fail you or forsake you.

So don't hesitate, procrastinate, or delay because you feel overwhelmed. Be strong and very courageous and start the work today.

∾ Pause and Sift ∾

Are you putting off a difficult task? Spend some time meditating on this verse. Let the truth that God is with you and that you have nothing to fear permeate your heart and mind.

Lord, would you give me the strength and courage that I need to do what you're asking of me, and the determination to see it through?

Learn to Breathe

*The Spirit of God has made me, and the
breath of the Almighty gives me life.*

JOB 33:4

The average adult takes between 17,280 and
23,040 breaths every day. Yet most of the time
we aren't even aware of this vital part of the
autonomic system operating in our bodies. The
miracle of life depends upon each breath.

In fact, most of us only really consider our
breathing when it noticeably changes. We might
hyperventilate when we are superanxious or
overly stressed, get winded when we overexert
ourselves, or struggle to breathe when we are
congested.

When you're extremely busy and constantly
running from one thing to the next, have you ever
caught yourself saying that you've barely stopped
to breathe? For a moment, you've reconnected to
an essential function that you need to exist.

It's not surprising that exercises and practices
which focus on controlling your breathing better,

such as Pilates and meditation, have become so popular in recent years. Learning to pause and breathe properly isn't as easy as it sounds!

Does your life seem frantic? Do you often feel tense, stressed out, or wound too tightly? Maybe you need to just stop and catch your breath.

Take my advice: Do it! If the pace of life seems to make you breathless right now, just pause and breathe deeply for a few moments. Ask God for his life-giving presence to fill each breath.

∾ Pause and Sift ∾

Take some slow, deep breaths and really think about God's breath filling you as you do. Breathe in his holy presence and breathe out the stress of the day.

Lord, thank you for every breath of life you give me. May I never take my life for granted. Help me honor you with every breath.

Less Is More

He cuts off every branch of mine that doesn't produce fruit, and he prunes the branches that do bear fruit so they will produce even more.

JOHN 15:2

Gardeners, arborists, and anyone who grows fruit know what happens when you prune a rosebush, an oak, or acres of fruit-bearing trees or vines. Pruning is a process of removing dead and lifeless things and reshaping wild and overgrown things in order to spur healthy growth.

In John 15:1, Jesus describes himself as the "true grapevine" and his Father as the gardener. He goes on to say that we are the branches his Father is pruning, and when we produce much fruit, we are Jesus' true disciples.

Although I'm not a gardener, I recognize the benefits of pruning in my life, realizing that oftentimes less is more. Less stuff, less spreading myself so thin, and fewer projects and commitments mean more time to spend with God, my family, and myself.

What about you? Maybe it's time to take a closer look at your life, too, and consider cutting back on some things and even cutting out others entirely.

Removing things from our lives that aren't adding any value or bearing any fruit helps keep us focused on what is most healthy and alive.

The process can be painful as we evaluate relationships, activities, possessions, commitments, and how we choose to prioritize our time—and then decide what to keep and what to eliminate. But I believe it's worth it for more fruit.

∾ Pause and Sift ∾

Take a quick inventory of your possessions and relationships as well as the activities on your calendar. Ask God to show you anything that needs to be cut out or cut back.

Lord, I've often believed the lie that more is better than less. Work in my heart and start a season of pruning that will lead to greater fruitfulness in my life.

Choose Celebration

I recommend having fun, because there
is nothing better for people in this world
than to eat, drink, and enjoy life.

ECCLESIASTES 8:15

Life can be hard sometimes, and it can really
wear down your soul. But isn't that more reason
to cultivate the practice of celebration?

My husband and I have recently walked
through a devastating season of recurrent miscarriages when we have cried, shouted, grieved,
wondered, worried, and wrestled with our questions to God while trying to process our loss.

All this was necessary. But then a time came
when we were done with feeling all that heartbreak and pain, and we decided to start celebrating again. We invited friends over for evenings
of eating, talking, and laughing together. And we
planned day trips and took weekend breaks away
to enjoy the fun side of life together as a family.

It takes determination to embrace goodness in
life when things don't work out as you'd like. We

followed King Solomon's wise advice to "enjoy life," and we've discovered that there is simply no better way.

Sometimes I catch myself wondering whether we should be doing something more spiritual instead. But God is part of these enjoyable moments just as much as any others. And when life is sometimes full of so much pain, don't we also need seasons of community and feasting and fun?

Celebration is such an important and underrated spiritual discipline that we can use both as worship and as part of our healing. Let's not sideline or undervalue this holy act.

∾ Pause and Sift ∾

Invite some friends over. If you don't cook or don't have time to, just provide snacks or order a pizza or takeout. It doesn't really matter what you serve as long as it comes with a supersize side of fun!

Lord, help me to practice celebration,
not just when life is going well but also
when I don't really feel like celebrating
but need to do it the most.

Need a Fill-Up?

The church is his body; it is made full and complete by
Christ, who fills all things everywhere with himself.

EPHESIANS 1:23

There's an awful lot in our lives that runs on almost empty.

My kitchen cupboards are often almost empty because I live in a household of hungry boys. My car's gas tank is often almost empty because I'm forever driving my family around. And my energy reserves are often almost empty because I'm cramming too much into one day.

This habit of running on almost empty can become much more problematic when it begins to affect our emotional and spiritual lives.

When we spend so much of our days organizing, managing, working for, looking after, feeding, cleaning up after, entertaining, serving, loving, helping, and giving to others, there's little left for ourselves. We don't allow enough refueling time to fill ourselves back up.

Is it any wonder that we sometimes are

snappy and irritable at the end of the day? The fact is that we simply can't give what we don't have.

Of course, we all have tiring days when we just need to take a break or turn in early. But sometimes that feeling of emptiness can also be a spiritual indicator that we are disconnected from the source of life.

Christ promised to fill all things everywhere with himself, so don't let yourself become depleted. Have confidence in his ability to fill all your empty places to overflowing.

∽ **Pause and Sift** ∾

Are there any areas of your life that feel empty right now? Simply bring them before God in prayer and ask him to replenish them again.

Lord, thank you that even when I feel empty or lacking, you promise to fill everything, everywhere. I invite you to come and fill my life with more of you today.

Quit Comparing

Jesus replied, "If I want him to remain alive until
I return, what is that to you? As for you, follow me."

JOHN 21:22

Have you fallen into the habit of comparing
yourself to others, only to find that you're slightly
lacking?

If so, what's your biggest hang-up? Your home,
your job, your income, your family, your ward-
robe, your weight, your popularity, your lifestyle,
your spirituality? Something else?

It's so easy to fall into a pattern of comparison
thinking and to end up believing that other people
are getting a better deal in life than us. But here's
the reality: Comparing is energy sapping and a
massive joy robber because it leaves us feeling
envious of others, fearful of missing out, and dissatisfied with what we have.

Social media only makes matters worse with
endless photos and posts that stir up jealousy. It's
too easy to forget that online profiles only allow
us to experience other people's lives through

carefully curated filters, edits, highlights, and "best moments."

I know comparison can often be subtle, and it's a really hard habit to break. But Jesus' words in today's verse still offer a timeless antidote: "What is that to you? As for you, follow me."

We will always find people to measure ourselves against. But really, what's the point? Just be grateful, joyful, and a good steward of what God has entrusted to you.

Don't waste time preoccupied with anyone else's journey, because Jesus simply asks you to follow him.

∾ Pause and Sift ∾

Each time you find yourself slipping into comparison mode this week, actively refocus your mind on your own blessings, talents, and God-given gifts instead.

Lord, help me not to get so easily
sidetracked by unhelpful comparisons
or with trying to be like anyone else.
I want to be someone who reflects
you in every aspect of my life.

Deal with Doubt

O LORD, how long will you forget me? Forever?
How long will you look the other way?

PSALM 13:1

Some of the most emotionally exhausting seasons in life can be when we're wrestling with doubts.

It can feel so isolating, as if you're the only person who's ever struggled with heavy questions in your heart. Scripture reminds us that doubting is nothing new. People have been exploring questions about faith for thousands of years.

I know it can feel scary to face difficult questions. And often we're reluctant to express them out loud. Maybe we're worried about where our doubts might lead us, or that we might upend someone else's faith too.

But God doesn't want us to shy away from difficult questions that are raised by our pain or suffering. Just look at the book of Psalms. It's full of wondering, questioning, and lament.

Jesus himself expressed his doubt out loud

when he hung on the cross and cried, "My God, my God, why have you abandoned me?" How mind-bending yet reassuring to know that even the divine would question the divine.

Ignoring difficult questions isn't spiritual. If we don't ask them, then how can we grow? Your faith isn't as flimsy or inflexible as you think. You can bend it, stretch it, and pull it apart. It's strong enough to withstand the pressure. God's Word holds up to scrutiny. His faithfulness has stood the test of time.

In the end, maybe your questions will actually prove to be the very thing that God uses to fortify your faith even more.

∾ Pause and Sift ∾

Do you have any difficult questions that you struggle to voice or share? Talk to God about them honestly today.

Lord, teach me to lean into my questions instead of avoiding them. Reveal your truth as I put my trust in you.

Rethink Self-Effort

It is not by force nor by strength, but by my
*Spirit, says the L*ORD *of Heaven's Armies.*

ZECHARIAH 4:6

When things go wrong in our lives, how many of
us immediately try to problem-solve and fix them
by ourselves? Self-effort is all about pushing,
hustling, jostling, persuading, and taking on even
more so we can get things done through sheer
willpower and steely determination.

Of course, there are some situations that call
for this kind of concentrated effort. But it's just
not a sustainable pace. It's like always driving
a car at Indy speeds, or sprinting for an entire
marathon. Eventually you will end up burning out
or resenting all the effort you had to put in.

Besides, why would we ever choose the limitations of our finite human ability when we could
harness the Holy Spirit's limitless power instead?
And even if self-effort produces results for a time,
it's still an exhausting and joyless way to live.
The truth is that self-effort is simply not the best

way to get things done, and it's definitely not the Kingdom way.

Maybe every now and then God allows us to struggle as a reminder that not everything is within our capabilities to fix or resolve. Sometimes we simply need to wait for God's Spirit to come and help us accomplish what we can't do on our own.

All it takes is for us to lay down our striving, our self-effort, our illusions of control and invite him to take the lead instead.

❧ Pause and Sift ❧

Spend a few moments quietly asking God to show you any areas in your life that you have tried to control through self-effort. Then surrender them to him.

Lord, I'm sorry that I often rely on self-effort when I could actually be empowered by you. Help me to give up my best-laid plans and choose to put my confidence in you.

More Than Positivity

*Humanly speaking, it is impossible. But
with God everything is possible.*

MATTHEW 19:26

There's some artwork hanging on my kitchen wall
that reads, "When life gives you lemons, make
lemonade." It reminds me to try to see the positive in every situation, even when things don't go
quite according to (my) plan.

A positive attitude is beneficial, but it only
takes you so far in life. These words of Jesus go
way beyond mere mind-over-matter determination or just trying to will something into happening. Faith is all about putting your confidence in
the One who is bigger than your circumstances.

We are finite, but we have a God who is infi-
nitely able. We are imperfect, but we have a God
who is perfect in every way. We are fallible and
limited in our humanity, but we have a God who is
infallible and wholly limitless.

He is omnipotent and omnipresent, all-
knowing and all-powerful. His touch can heal the

sick, make blind eyes see, and even raise the dead back to life. And his words can bring light out of darkness and call nothingness into being.

The Bible isn't just another self-help book on how to get more out of your life; it's the living and active Word of God that reveals his heart, and reading it strengthens our faith.

Positive thinking can help change your outlook on impossible situations, but the supernatural power of our God can actually make the impossible happen.

∾ Pause and Sift ∾

Are you facing a difficult situation right now?
Spend some time meditating on the truth
that nothing is impossible with God, and let
that truth begin to build your faith.

———————————

Lord, help me live in the knowledge that
everything is possible when I put my faith in
you, despite how my circumstances might
look or how discouraged I may feel.

Sleep Well

When you lie down, you will not be afraid;
when you lie down, your sleep will be sweet.

PROVERBS 3:24, NIV

How well do you sleep? Are you out as soon as your head hits the pillow, or does it take you a while to unwind?

And once you have drifted off into slumber, do you sleep until morning, or do you have a restless night?

In one study, more than half of the US adults surveyed said they struggle to get a good night's sleep at least once a week. Psychophysiological issues such as stress, anxiety, and the inability to switch off from the day are said to cause around 70 percent of these sleep problems.

You may have resigned yourself to simply putting up with poor sleep habits, but how well you sleep really matters. It affects your energy, concentration, productivity, mood, and even your health.

So what can you do about it? You can allow

yourself more time to wind down from your day and improve your sleep by ditching electronic devices. Make sure your sleep environment is comfortable, dark, and quiet. Also, are you due for a new mattress or pillow?

Most of all, you can spend a few minutes reflecting on the events that may have unfolded and give any niggling issues or concerns over to God before you lie down. He promises to give you peaceful, sweet sleep.

❧ Pause and Sift ❧

Give your thoughts and worries to God each night just before you lie down to sleep—either in silent or spoken prayer or by recording them in a journal.

Lord, your Word says that you offer sweet rest; but sometimes I struggle to fall asleep. Would you show me how to decompress from my day and embrace your peace as I go to sleep?

Partner with Him

*The Son can do nothing by himself. He does
only what he sees the Father doing.*

JOHN 5:19

I often find myself questioning whether I'm really
doing enough to grow God's Kingdom. But today's
verse reassures me that my service doesn't need
to be elaborate or difficult. All God is asking of
me is to live in close step with him and to join in
whenever I see my Father doing something.

The truth is that serving God doesn't need
to be complicated or time-consuming. It doesn't
even need to take you out of your way. It all starts
with just loving the people God puts in front of
you in everyday ways.

It could be as simple as befriending another
mom while waiting for your kids at the bus stop
or taking the time to chat with that shy person
in your office who often gets overlooked. It could
be showing some interest in the cashier who is
scanning your items at the grocery store checkout

or sending a little text and prayer to someone in your life who is having a hard time.

And if it doesn't sound particularly difficult, that's because it's not. All it takes is making yourself available and being willing to partner with God whenever the opportunity arises.

You personally carry God's presence and his love into the middle of ordinary situations. Never doubt how powerful and life changing that can be for you and the people you encounter.

∾ Pause and Sift ∾

Ask God for a chance to partner with him in a normal, everyday moment in your life this week.

Lord, help me to live with an open heart and
open eyes, because I don't want to miss
out on any opportunity to join you in what
you're doing in the world around me.

Worth Your Time

Let your "Yes" be "Yes," and your "No," "No."

MATTHEW 5:37, NKJV

I don't know whether you've noticed the huge swing toward people being late in recent years.

You're waiting for someone in a café when suddenly a text from your friend buzzes through telling you she is delayed. And so you're left sipping a latte alone.

We've probably all been there at times, on both sides of that scenario. I'm not criticizing anyone for being genuinely delayed by the unexpected, because sometimes life throws you a surprise curveball. But if you repeatedly end up running late or letting people down with last-minute cancellations, then chances are your life is overbooked.

It's easy to categorize poor time management or bad organization as a practical issue rather than a spiritual one. But I believe Jesus' words in today's verse hit home on both fronts.

"Let your 'Yes' be 'Yes,' and your 'No,' 'No'"

means not procrastinating or putting off until tomorrow those decisions that you could actually make today. And it means honoring your word—not agreeing to do something when you know you won't be able to give it the time it really deserves.

But most of all, I think it means not treating other people as if their time were less important than yours.

Are you serious about following the example of Jesus in every area of your life? If so, be decisive, be dependable and committed to keeping your word, and practice being the kind of friend to others that you would want to have.

∽ Pause and Sift ∾

Review your schedule for the coming weeks. Is there anything you need to cancel or rearrange, or any protected time that you need to add in?

———————————————

Lord, I know I need to be more intentional with my time and more mindful about meaning it when I say yes or no. I want to honor you with how I choose to spend each day.

See Things Differently

Take delight in the LORD, and he will give you your heart's desires.

PSALM 37:4

I love this verse. But I used to interpret it wrong.

For years I thought it meant that if you delighted yourself in God, he would give you pretty much whatever you asked for, like a holy Santa Claus.

But the problem was that whenever something I really wanted didn't happen fast enough, I thought I needed to do more "spiritual stuff" in order to somehow twist his arm and get it.

So when getting my dream job, finding the right guy, or whatever else I desired didn't materialize within a reasonable time frame, I would find myself questioning my faith. Why was God withholding something good from me? Wasn't I delighting in him enough? Hadn't I put in enough fervent hours of prayer or selfless good works?

It has taken me years of wrestling with disappointment to realize that this kind of thinking is totally flawed. God isn't a spiritual vending machine; you can't insert spiritual tokens and then select whatever you want from him with the push of a button. A relationship with God can't be treated as if it were another consumer transaction.

When we delight ourselves in the Lord, the desires of our hearts will naturally begin to fall more in line with his. Our perspectives will begin to change. Our priorities will become his priorities, and we'll begin to discover that all our hearts' desires are best satisfied in him.

∾ Pause and Sift ∾

If you have an unfulfilled desire in your heart right now, simply release it to God in prayer and redetermine to pursue the Giver, not the gifts.

Lord, I'm sorry that I sometimes approach you for what I want rather than because of who you are. Help me to discover the joy of simply being in your presence.

Find Your Crew

*Two people are better off than one, for they
can help each other succeed. If one person
falls, the other can reach out and help.*

ECCLESIASTES 4:9-10

We're the most technologically connected
generation ever but also the most relationally
disconnected.

In fact, almost half of those who responded
to a 2018 online survey reported regularly feeling
alone. How can that be? Have we settled for the
illusion of connectedness over genuine community, breadth of reach over depth of intimacy, and
just being known *about* over really being known?

These verses remind me that we really need
one another. We are relational beings, created in
the image of a relational God, designed to thrive
best together.

Choosing to prioritize people and intentionally
investing in a community is worth doing, even
when it feels hard.

Seek out a regular group in your church,

neighborhood, or workplace. Enroll in a class or start a new hobby. Or better yet, why not build a community yourself? Initiate some coffee dates with others, or playdates if you have kids. Open up your home and your heart.

If you don't immediately click with someone, don't worry. Persevere until you find your group. And once you have, love them hard and don't let go.

Chances are that you will really need them someday, and they will need you too.

Two people certainly are better than one . . . but a whole community is even better still!

∾ Pause and Sift ∾

If you haven't yet found your crew, ask God to show you who they are. Or if you already are part of one, ask him for an idea to help strengthen your group's connection and impact.

Lord, thank you for the friends who have blessed me throughout my life. Show me how to be the kind of friend to others that I would want to have myself.

Watch and Wait

*Each morning I bring my requests to
you and wait expectantly.*

PSALM 5:3

One of the most important principles I learned
while studying marketing and communications is
that communication is only effective when it's a
two-way process.

If you send an email, you can't assume it was
received. You have to wait for a response to be
sure. Yet how often do we approach our prayer
life as if it were a one-way conversation?

We make our requests known to God, and
then off we go with our day. I wonder if how long
we are willing to wait for a reply says a lot about
how much we really expect an answer from God.

He might be just about to dispatch the answer
to us, only to discover that we're not even watching or waiting for one to arrive. Instead we have
already rushed off to start organizing our own
plan B.

How ridiculous! It's like ordering an item from

Amazon Prime, then immediately borrowing it from a friend because you don't really think the package will show up.

Maybe that's why some of the prophets in the Bible talk about building watchtowers; if we don't wait expectantly for an answer from the Lord, we might miss what he wants to send into our lives.

God's responses to our requests might not always look exactly as we had hoped or arrive within our designated time frame; but we can always be sure that he hears us when we pray and that an answer will follow.

✑ Pause and Sift ✑

How can you build a "watchtower" for God over your heart and your life this week?

_____

Lord, I'm sorry that sometimes I pray only as a gesture, without any real faith that you will answer. Teach me how to wait eagerly and expectantly for you.

The Power of
Self-Reflection

*When Jesus saw him and knew he had
been ill for a long time, he asked him,
"Would you like to get well?"*

JOHN 5:6

How am I? Pose that simple question to yourself.

Maybe you're feeling great right now, but if
your answer is "Just okay" or "Could be better,"
I can assure you God is listening and cares.

If you're feeling physically run-down, fighting
illness, or struggling emotionally today, know that
he wants to make you well, just as he did for the
lame man Jesus addressed in today's verse.

Instead of immediately healing the man, Jesus
first asked him a question: "Would you like to
get well?" Jesus' question seems strange to me,
implying that a healing outcome depended partly
on the lame man's own choice.

What point do you think Jesus was trying to
make? Possibly the man had become so used to

his condition that he just accepted it as part of who he was, or perhaps he no longer expected healing or even recognized his need.

What about you? Have you lost your desire to be more than just okay, believing this is the life you've been given? Aren't we all guilty of this attitude sometimes?

Practicing regular self-reflection is important. When we don't take the time to check on how we're doing, it can be easy to miss how physically or emotionally unwell we have become.

Maybe Jesus is holding out his healing hand to you today. Are you ready to admit that you need to be made well?

∾ Pause and Sift ∾

Be more aware of how you are feeling. Ask yourself How am I? *and* What can I do about it? *Try to make this self-reflection a regular habit.*

Lord, thank you that you care about my health and want me to be well. Help me recognize when something is wrong and quickly seek help.

Try Laughing

He will once again fill your mouth with
laughter and your lips with shouts of joy.

JOB 8:21

I've heard it said that laughter is the sound of the soul dancing, which I think is both beautifully poetic and true. Laughter is such an underrated but important spiritual practice.

Have you ever considered asking God to give you more laughter when you're facing difficulties? Maybe that kind of request seems a bit too self-indulgent, too silly, or too frivolous to be spiritual. But laughter is an amazing gift from God.

Did you know that laughing is scientifically proven to reduce feelings of stress and improve our mood? What's more, it can actually increase our ability to cope with physical pain and illness and increase our immunity.

In fact, tests have shown that watching just fifteen minutes of comedy can make us 10 percent more resistant to pain. How incredible is that? It seems that saying about laughter being the best medicine is really true after all! It is even likely based on Scripture. Proverbs 17:22 says, "A cheerful heart is good medicine."

I know that we live in a world where we don't always feel happy or experience laugh-out-loud moments; but what if we could learn to laugh a bit more often—even in the midst of the mediocre and mundane?

And what if we intentionally pursue joyfulness, even when we're facing difficulty or pain? How different we would feel if we actually asked God to fill our mouths with laughter and our lips with joy!

∾ Pause and Sift ∾

Seek out joy triggers in your life: stand-up comedians, funny films, or just friends who laugh a lot and know how to practice joy well.

Lord, sometimes I allow situations to steal my joy too quickly; I simply don't value laughter enough. So today, please bless me with lots of laugh-out-loud moments.

Refuse to Rush

There is a time ... for every
purpose and for every work.

ECCLESIASTES 3:17, KJV

We have more leisure time today than any previous generation, yet many of us still feel rushed. How can that possibly be? Maybe all those time-saving gadgets we've accumulated just allow us to squeeze even more into already full days.

Often that sense of urgency happens when we try to take on too much in too short a time frame. But what if we really learned to slow down, take on less, and live out the timeless wisdom in this verse?

There is a time for every purpose and every work.

Let me clarify what that means.

Not everything is needed today.

Not everything is needed at all.

I know it can be hard to determine what is truly important when we are bombarded with endless distractions and diversions buzzing on our phones. But if we don't, we'll only wear ourselves out trying to do everything, and we'll do it badly because we're spreading ourselves too thin.

Living in this continual state of hurriedness isn't how we were designed to exist. We were created to live more present in each moment so we can enjoy the freedom Jesus promised.

It's a whole lot easier to stop rushing and to start trusting that there's a season and time for everything when your priorities line up with God's.

∿ Pause and Sift ∿

Are you putting unnecessary pressure on yourself by taking on too much at once? Practice prioritizing, and focus on accomplishing just one important task this coming week.

Lord, help me evaluate the importance of my commitments. Show me how to assess my priorities so they more fully align with yours.

Stay Present

This is the day the LORD has made.
We will rejoice and be glad in it.

PSALM 118:24

Have you ever been physically present with someone and yet somewhere else in your head?

It's perfectly possible to be so self-absorbed
and preoccupied with problems that you miss
everything that's good in the here and now. Being
present means noticing and savoring all the rich
beauty and detail within each unfolding moment
rather than being distracted by ruminations
on the past or worries about the future. And it
means holding space for deeper connections with
others as you seek to give them your complete,
undivided attention.

When your life is monotonous or full of difficulty or pain, it's especially tempting to mentally
check out. Instead of facing challenges, it's more
appealing to escape into the world of Candy
Crush Saga or binge-watch shows on Hulu
instead.

But here's the thing: When you aren't fully present, you can overlook some of your greatest blessings, or even miss what God wants to teach you right now.

Instead of daydreaming about somewhere else you'd rather be, choose to embrace exactly where God has placed you.

There's nothing more sacred than spending each of the ordinary moments unfolding in your life with that person sitting in front of you.

∾ Pause and Sift ∾

Instead of multitasking, be mindful of the situation in front of you and give your full attention to those you are with. Put away your phone and look them in the eye.

Lord, would you give me fresh grace for today? Help me to stay focused on the here and now and to find contentment in my present, whatever circumstances I may face—because today is your gift to me.

Embrace the Journey

He guides me along the right
paths for his name's sake.

PSALM 23:3, NIV

After being caught in traffic, have you ever
decided to take a detour around the congestion,
ultimately making the situation worse? Or have
you ever boarded a plane, only to sit on the run-
way for hours?

Is there anything more frustrating than being
stuck in the middle of a journey, unable to get
where you want to be?

Yet in the Bible God often seems more interested in who his people are becoming during the
journey than whether—or when—they arrive at
the final destination. Just look at the story of the
Israelites after God rescued them from slavery in
Egypt. If everything had gone as planned, the trip
from Mount Sinai to the Promised Land should
have only taken them eleven days. Instead, they
ended up wandering in the wilderness for forty
years!

I used to think of most of my life as a race to arrive at the next destination—my career, ministry, marriage, or parenting. But when my journey to each of these destinations unfolded far more slowly and indirectly than I expected, I began to realize that God was more concerned with how closely I traveled with him than in how fast I arrived.

And even when I did arrive, I quickly realized that none of those places were the final destination. After all, God doesn't call his people to settle but to keep walking with him.

∾ Pause and Sift ∾

Are you restless to arrive somewhere or at risk of settling too soon? Simply recommit to embrace the journey with God today.

Lord, help me to remember that every destination here on earth is just a temporary stop on my lifelong journey toward my ultimate heavenly home.

Listen to Your Body

A peaceful heart leads to a healthy body.
PROVERBS 14:30

Often we can fool ourselves into thinking that we are handling stressful situations well. But sometimes our bodies give us away.

We might spend a restless night tossing and turning; have tightness in our shoulders, aching muscles, or sweaty palms; experience panic; or even feel run down or become ill.

At times these physical signs can be an indication that we are struggling in some way; that we may need to slow down, listen to our bodies more, and practice better self-care.

Self-care is not just an add-on to try and squeeze extra activities into an overfull life. It's about recognizing that the gospel is holistic and that Jesus came to set every part of us free.

A while ago I had a painful trapped nerve in my shoulder. Physical therapy initially helped, but the problem would sporadically flare up again—usually during periods of intense emotional stress, such as after each of my miscarriages.

In the end, I found relief through combining the physical with the spiritual: giving the source of my stress over to God in prayer but also using low-impact stretching and relaxation techniques to help relieve the tension.

Today's verse reminds us not to compartmentalize or separate our physical health from our emotional and spiritual lives. Both are intrinsically connected, and we must be aware when one or the other needs extra-attentive care.

∾ Pause and Sift ∾

Try some simple relaxation techniques to help you focus on listening to your body. There are lots of free apps to get you started at home.

Lord, help me to get better at listening to what my body might be trying to tell me, and faster at doing something about it.

Feast with Him

You prepare a feast for me
in the presence of my enemies.

PSALM 23:5

Today's verse, taken from the beloved Twenty-third Psalm, has always seemed weird to me. Why would someone prepare a meal for their loved ones in the midst of a battlefield? I wouldn't!

And I don't want God to prepare a meal *for me* in the presence of my enemies either! I would much rather that he defeat and destroy them all first, and then we could enjoy a quiet, peaceful meal afterward.

But God clearly doesn't see it that way. He says that while we are still facing adversity or feeling under attack, he wants to sit and feast with us. He isn't rattled by the presence of our enemies at all, so we don't need to be either.

Still, why a feast? Whenever I take the time to prepare a meal for family or friends, it's a mark of my care for them, as well as a practical source of refreshment and nourishment. But it's also a place for conversing, reconnecting, and enjoying life together.

In this psalm, God is inviting us to experience all those things at his table, too: his care, his provision, his strengthening, and his joy when we're weary from the fight.

But most of all, it's an invitation to simply spend time in his presence. When we rest in him and feast with him, we are empowered to face life's battles.

∾ Pause and Sift ∾

Set aside some time for celebrating and feasting in God's presence, regardless of what else may be happening in your life.

Lord, I choose to take a seat at your table and to indulge in your goodness today, even as my enemies still surround me.

Let Go

*But forget all that—it is nothing
compared to what I am going to do.*

ISAIAH 43:18

Letting go of past hurts can be extremely difficult,
but holding on to something that you can't change
or undo can end up hurting you even more.

Are you struggling to let go of something right
now? Perhaps it's a previous relationship that
broke your heart or a grudge you still hold against
someone who wronged you. Maybe you're harboring guilt over a past mistake or you're deeply disappointed about something that just didn't work
out as you'd hoped.

Often when we fail to deal with and release
painful things, we end up revisiting or reliving
them over and over in our minds. And if your
heart is cluttered with old disappointments or
pain, how can there be any space for finding joy
in something new?

Letting go of emotional situations that are
over and done with isn't a simple process. But it's

much easier when you realize that God is in control and you can trust him with your future.

So if you're still clinging to something that's damaging your mind and heart, let go and let God set you free from any emotional hold the past still has over you. Let go and let him give you something better.

∼ Pause and Sift ∼

Make a conscious decision to let go of anything that has already let go of you. Take some proactive steps to help you move forward. For example, throw away any unhelpful reminders or stop checking that person's social media so you can stop revisiting the past in your head.

Lord, help me to let go of anything in my past that may be holding me back from my future. I open my hands and release those painful memories to you, and I open my heart to the new things you have for me.

Fight Decision Fatigue

How long will you waver between two opinions?

1 KINGS 18:21, NIV

Do you sometimes stand in a grocery store aisle and feel your stress level rise as you look at all the choices? You wonder, *Which brand is the best value, the healthiest option, or the most environmentally friendly choice?*

In 1976 there were just nine thousand different products in the average store, but less than twenty years later, there were about thirty thousand. And you literally have to mentally filter out thousands of options every time you buy a few groceries. No wonder we struggle with decision fatigue!

It's easy to feel paralyzed by indecision or become anxious about selecting the wrong items. But prolonged procrastination can lead to inaction and be just as damaging as making an imperfect decision.

So how do we stop wavering back and forth and become purposeful? Some decisions in life are pretty black or white because God has already given us clear instructions in the Bible.

But for many other day-to-day decisions, there may not be a clear right or wrong. Instead, God offers us personal choice, which often feels much harder but helps us to grow in discernment.

If we genuinely seek to honor God in all we do, how can our decisions ever be wrong? Even poor ones made in good faith present an opportunity to learn. Maybe God is more interested in our growth than in us always being right the first time.

∾ Pause and Sift ∾

Are there any looming decisions you have been putting off? Prayerfully invite the Holy Spirit to guide you; then move on with your day. Return to the decision later and see what new perspectives have emerged.

Lord, I know I often can be indecisive or worry about getting things wrong. Help me learn to submit my decisions to you and then to step out with confidence.

Accept the Bittersweet

Rejoice with those who rejoice;
mourn with those who mourn.

ROMANS 12:15, NIV

I love the sentiment of today's verse, but I think it's a tough calling too. Whenever you have reason to rejoice, it's hard to remember what it's like to mourn, and when you're in the midst of mourning, it's hard to stomach those who are rejoicing.

Life is full of these confusing tensions and juxtaposing emotions, isn't it? A wedding celebration with a mention of a recently lost parent, a family engagement alongside a divorce, someone landing their dream job while another endures weekly drudgery, a baby announcement after news of a miscarriage.

But this is life in all its rich shades of color: the pleasure and the pain, the joy and the despair, the beauty and the brokenness, the bitter and the sweet. God invites us to embrace it all.

When we're still waiting for something to materialize, or when we're grieving something that's been lost, someone else's elation can really be grating. Likewise, when we're rewarded for an achievement or hitting an emotional high, someone else's sadness can feel like a real buzzkill.

To live the life of love that Jesus called us to, we must be willing to sit with people in their pain and suffering as well as share in their moments of happiness and celebration.

It can be messy and feel awkward at times, but whenever we choose to meet people exactly where they are, more of Christ is revealed through us.

∾ Pause and Sift ∾

Is someone in your life either rejoicing or mourning right now? Consider how you can support them and even journey through that season with them.

Lord, help me to show more empathy to others around me and to offer understanding. Help me live a life marked by your love.

Be Smart with Your Phone

*You say, "I am allowed to do anything"—
but not everything is beneficial.*

1 CORINTHIANS 10:23

Are you controlling your phone, or is your phone controlling you? According to some studies, the average American checks their mobile phone eighty times a day and spends around three hours browsing its small screen.

Maybe we just don't notice the amount of time we're wasting by mindlessly scrolling because it's broken up into lots of short, repeated actions.

I don't have anything against technology. I use it as much as anyone. But that statistic equates to twenty-one hours a week—forty-five full days a year—that could be used more beneficially. #justsaying!

Part of the problem is that phone apps are designed to be addictive, to keep us glued to our screens by hooking us back in with alerts. The more we scroll, the more time and money we tend to spend.

So exactly how much is too much time on your phone? The Bible obviously doesn't give us a specific stipulation, but the apostle Paul says in today's verse that everything is permissible but not necessarily beneficial.

Stop and ask yourself, *Is my phone use making me more connected to others or more isolated and antisocial? Is it making me better informed or just more prone to wasting time?*

Because if, like me, you often find yourself complaining that there aren't enough hours in the day, then maybe you need to take a serious look at your phone habits.

∾ Pause and Sift ∾

Establish some rules for using your mobile phone: Set up a communal docking point for your family, make mealtimes phone-free, or agree upon a shutoff time for all mobile devices.

Lord, I know that too often I can't put my phone down because I'm certain I'll miss something important. Please help me be more disciplined with my time.

Wilderness Walking

Who is this sweeping in from the
desert, leaning on her lover?
SONG OF SONGS 8:5

Have you ever been through a wilderness time?
If so, you're not alone. References to a desert or
wilderness occur nearly four hundred times in
the Bible and often are associated with periods of
disorientation, wandering, temptation, desolation,
or difficulty. Even Jesus spent forty days and
nights being tested by Satan in the wilderness.

Without a doubt, the wilderness experience is
part of every Christian's journey—if not physically,
then metaphorically.

It's easy to be pessimistic during a wilderness
season because it's a lonely and barren experience. But what if there were some purpose, or
even goodness, to be found there too?

After all, the desert can be a place for
encountering God, a place where he speaks with
greater clarity or reveals himself to his people in
new ways.

Sometimes I wonder why God allows us to undergo wilderness times. But how much growing and changing and listening to God do we really do when everything is fine? It's usually during difficulty or testing that I tend to search for his presence the most.

Today's verse offers us a beautiful picture of what a desert experience can do for us—it creates a deeper dependence on God and fresh intimacy with him. When we emerge from the parched landscape, we're changed—because we leaned in closer to him.

∾ Pause and Sift ∾

What areas of your life are barren or desertlike right now? What can you do to draw closer to God through them rather than pulling away?

Lord, I long to know you more. Teach me how to lean in to you, not just in times of wilderness but also throughout every day of every season.

Renew Your Strength

Those who trust in the LORD will find new strength.
They will soar high on wings like eagles. They will run
and not grow weary. They will walk and not faint.

ISAIAH 40:31

As a parent of a young child, I still readily recall how tiring the baby phase can be. It is one of the most testing, long-term kinds of exhaustion I've ever experienced.

When your kid isn't sleeping night after night, for months on end, fatigue quickly becomes the norm. Too often, in that fog of tiredness, I found myself just gulping strong coffee and grabbing some sugary snacks to help power me through.

Today I no longer have the excuse of a newborn in the house, yet too often I still choose to labor on in my own strength, only to end up depleted of energy and giving the very worst of myself to my family, who mean the most to me.

Self-sufficiency can be a hard habit to break, whatever life stage you are in. But what if we actually take these words of Isaiah seriously?

What if, instead of relying on caffeine or sugar, we act like we really believe that God is the source of our strength? When we start struggling and feeling weary, what if we ask him to come and renew us?

We'd probably discover that we feel healthier, less grumpy, and rejuvenated for the day; and we would likely experience more of God's peace as well.

∾ Pause and Sift ∾

Whenever you find yourself yawning or complaining about being tired, ask God out loud or silently to renew your strength right in that moment.

Lord, you promise to give strength to the weary when they put their trust in you. Help me not to be so self-sufficient that I forget your promises. I want you to be my source and my strength.

Self-Help or God's Help?

Is anyone among you in trouble? Let them pray.

JAMES 5:13, NIV

If I want to get from A to B, I can ask my GPS to guide me. If I require some information, I can consult Siri, Alexa, or Google Assistant. And when I need advice, I can just phone, text, or message a friend.

The amount of self-help information and advice we have available to us seems to grow by the minute. But I wonder if this has sometimes caused us to be slower to pray and ask God for help.

Like many women in my generation, I grew up on a heavy diet of feminism, equality, and girl power. I learned how to aim high, believe in myself, and be a strong and independent modern woman—all good and empowering aspirations.

But maybe somewhere along the line we also unintentionally internalized the message that to be strong is to be self-sufficient. This can be a massive stumbling block to faith because it prevents us from acknowledging or admitting our desperate need for God.

Sometimes we need a few challenges to nudge us into asking others for help, to remind us that we're not quite as invincible as we think.

Let's face it: We simply can't do everything by ourselves. And we don't need to, thankfully, because God freely offers us his help.

∾ Pause and Sift ∾

The next time you face a problem, challenge yourself to seek God's help first before you try any other avenue. When you do this regularly, you'll find yourself automatically turning to him instead of considering him a last resort.

Lord, I often struggle with trying to fix everything myself, and I only think to pray as a last resort. Help me become better at recognizing my limitations and quicker to ask for your help.

Stop the Hustle

Martha was distracted by all the
preparations that had to be made.

LUKE 10:40, NIV

Sometimes staying busy can be easier than
choosing to just be still.

We live in a world that's obsessed with the
pursuit of the perfect. And when we're constantly
chasing that elusive notion, there's always something still left to be done. We continue pushing,
planning, preparing, making, shaping, fixing,
cleaning, styling things—always trying to spin
more plates.

Deep down we know that achieving perfection
is impossible, and yet we work harder to attain
it. Striving for "better" is exhausting! The truth is
that "good enough" will usually do just fine.

Maybe a lot of our busyness is well-
intentioned, such as serving other people, just
as Martha was doing. But even noble acts can
sometimes cause us to miss the opportunity

to meaningfully connect with God or others around us.

We're not called to a life of überorganization and external perfection but to prioritize our relationship with God. Sometimes he might ask us to stop everything we're doing and just sit at his feet.

So if you're feeling weary from the never-ending hustle, maybe Jesus wants to gently speak these words to you today: "You are worried and upset about many things, but few things are needed—or indeed only one."

∾ Pause and Sift ∾

Focus on the important instead of what's pressing you today. Let some of the small stuff slide. Set aside some extended time in your day to spend sitting at Jesus' feet and learning from him.

Lord, I'm sorry that I often let my preoccupation with many unimportant things distract me from the one thing that matters. Today I choose to prioritize the better thing, which is sitting at your feet and spending time with you.

Always Aware

Surely the LORD is in this place, and
I wasn't even aware of it!

GENESIS 28:16

It's one thing to know that God is always with us,
but it's another thing to encounter his presence
in a tangible way.

Jacob had been dreaming about a stairway
between heaven and earth, with angels going up
and down. For most of us, such striking visions
don't happen often.

When Jacob woke up, he said, "Surely the
LORD is in this place, and I wasn't even aware
of it!" God hadn't suddenly appeared from out
of nowhere; he was actually there all along, but
Jacob simply hadn't noticed.

Could the same be true for us? I wonder how
many of us are living in those thin spaces where
God's presence is very near, but we fail to have
any real awareness of it because we are living too
frantically.

Some Christians spend their entire lives

searching for physical manifestations of God's presence or that next mountaintop experience, only to miss the fact that he is already with us in the ordinary moments.

I don't want to risk missing God's presence in my home, my workplace, or my neighborhood simply because I failed to take a few moments to connect with him.

Choosing to remember he is with us as we go about our daily routines, and taking ten to twenty seconds here and there to whisper a few words to him, can reshape our entire day.

⁓ Pause and Sift ⁓

When you awake each morning, acknowledge that God's presence is with you. Make it a regular habit throughout your day as well.

Lord, make me more consciously aware of your constant presence. Help me to discover you in the ordinary places of my life.

Work Joyfully

Work willingly at whatever you do, as though you
were working for the Lord rather than for people.

COLOSSIANS 3:23

Do you ever get that sinking feeling on Sunday night that turns into the Monday-morning blues? Work is such a drag sometimes, isn't it?

I am fortunate to work in a marketing career that I studied for and chose to pursue, but even so, some days it can still feel like an endless drudgery of paperwork, spreadsheets, and meetings.

If I'm honest, too often I can treat my workday like an unwelcome hindrance keeping me from all the other things I'd rather be doing, such as socializing with friends, being with family, or serving God in my community.

The Bible paints a very different picture of work—as a blessing, not a curse. In fact, in Genesis, God calls Adam to work alongside him in bringing order to his creation. Work has always been part of God's divine purpose for our lives.

I know work doesn't always feel purposeful, especially when we're in jobs that we really don't love. But rather than complaining, feeling negative, or seeking new opportunities every time we feel frustrated or bored, what if we invite God into our work instead?

Ambition isn't a bad thing, but God doesn't ask us to continually ladder-climb or career-hop in search of the "perfect" position. He calls us to serve him wholeheartedly through what he has given us to do.

∾ Pause and Sift ∾

Pray for your work today, whether in the office or at home. Ask God to give you renewed vision for the tasks before you and the role he has placed you in.

Lord, I am determined to give my very best to whatever work I find myself doing today, remembering that the most important thing is doing it in a way which honors you.

Know His Peace

Peace I leave with you; my peace I give you. I do not give to you as the world gives. Do not let your hearts be troubled and do not be afraid.

JOHN 14:27, NIV

Just a brief scan of the news headlines in the morning often can leave us reeling and feeling like we're carrying the weight of the world on our shoulders: international conflicts, natural disasters, global pandemics, political uprisings, economic downturns, human atrocities, climate change, and more.

Maybe there's a direct correlation between the amount of information we consume and the level of anxiety that we feel.

I'm not advocating burying our heads in the sand; it's important to stay informed about what's happening in the world. But don't you find it interesting that the one thing Jesus promised to leave his disciples with was peace? Not wisdom, or knowledge, or power, or even love—but peace.

Clearly Jesus knew his followers would need

it. And if they needed it then, how much more do
we need to know that peace today, in this beautiful but broken, anxiety-inducing world?

Practices like relaxation and mindfulness
can be useful to help us manage the pressures of
modern life, but they only go so far. Jesus offers
us his peace, which isn't circumstantial or temporary. His peace is unshakable, unchangeable, and
immovable because it's based on who he is and
what he has already done for us.

∽ Pause and Sift ∽

Where do you need more of God's peace
in your life? Reflect on who God is and
experience peace in a deeper way.

Lord, your Word says that you know all my
anxious thoughts. Today I invite you to come
and exchange them for your peace.

Enjoy Each Season

For everything there is a season, a time
for every activity under heaven.

ECCLESIASTES 3:1

Are you enjoying the season you are in right now?

Personally, I'm a real summer person. I just love the opportunities for sociability and spending time outdoors that warmer weather brings: barbecues and picnics, lounging by the pool and working in the garden, and enjoying long, balmy evenings together.

If I could live in summer weather year-round, I think I probably would. Whenever colder, darker autumn days begin to push summer off the calendar, it always feels like it's happening too soon.

But the truth is that I can't waste months of every year feeling negative or wishing that I could be relaxing in the warmth of the sun on a beach. So this year, I have decided to embrace the changing seasons and focus on all that's good in each of them.

Isn't this the best way to get through any

season of life that we don't like? Instead of resisting or resenting it, what if we actually looked for the good that exists in each one?

There are seasons that we all love to be in—seasons of breakthrough, celebration, and joy. But there are also more challenging ones too.

Maybe God created the changing seasons etched in nature as a physical reminder that no season of life lasts forever. Everything has a beginning and an end, and he promises to make everything beautiful again in his time.

∾ Pause and Sift ∾

Do something seasonal this week, however small or large. Think of it as a way to embrace the present season of life you're in.

Lord, thank you for this present season of life that I find myself in. Help me to approach it with greater intentionality, eager to grasp everything you have planned for me in it.

Tune In

I called you so often, but you wouldn't come.
I reached out to you, but you paid no attention.

PROVERBS 1:24

My husband often jokes that I love my mobile phone more than him because I pay more attention to it. I do understand the point he's trying to make: Love thrives on attentiveness. And it makes me wonder, *How often does God feel I'm overlooking him too?*

How often have I tuned in to a podcast or TV show instead of his voice? How often have I chosen to talk to a friend rather than seek God directly for his guidance about a problem? And how often have I chosen to listen to the news or check my social media feeds instead of hearing what he has to say about my day?

How we use our time, whether intentionally or unintentionally, always reflects what takes precedence in our hearts. Although I often say I want God's presence to be more real in my life, I don't always make it a priority in my day.

Still, God calls and reaches out to me, just like a dear friend or lover would, waiting for me to give him my full attention. What an incredible thought!

I have never been good at having a regular quiet time. But there is simply no "one size fits all" for spending time with Jesus.

The truth is, it doesn't really matter when, where, or how we choose to connect with God during our day; it only matters that we do, and that we give him our full attention.

∽ Pause and Sift ∽

What helps you feel well-connected to God? Music, meditation, silence, running, venturing out into nature, or something else? Whatever it is, do more of it this week.

Lord, I really want to experience more of you in my life. Help me to prioritize my relationship with you and make space for you during my day.

Release Your Worry

Give all your worries and cares to
God, for he cares about you.

1 PETER 5:7

Do you ever wake up with a sense of dread about the day ahead, thinking about how much you have to get through? Or when you lie down to sleep, do you find your mind racing, unable to switch off? Me, too, sometimes.

In fact, anxiety disorders affect about one in five adults in America today, and many more of us live in a continuous state of low-level worry in our overstretched, overcrammed lives.

This verse reminds us that we don't need to live like this. We don't need to silently suffer with anxious thoughts; God wants us to give all our worries to him. He lovingly offers to carry the heavy load for us.

And yet often we are still weighed down. Part of the problem may be how easy it is to fool ourselves into thinking that we have given each and every care over to God when, in reality, we just keep picking them back up and trying to control the situation ourselves.

Sometimes we can even end up "prayer-worrying"—bringing the same anxious thoughts to God over and over again through our prayers. Is that truly trusting him?

God doesn't invite us to lay down the same burdens continually. He asks us to give them to him and leave them in his care.

～ Pause and Sift ～

Is something worrying you, weighing you down, or making you anxious today? Give it to God in prayer. If you find yourself tempted to worry again, just remember that God has already got it!

Lord, I choose to hand all my worries over to you today. Help me to resist the urge to pick them back up again as I trust in your care for me.

Unleash
Your Creativity

In the beginning God created the heavens and the earth.

GENESIS 1:1

The very first words in the Bible tell us that in the beginning, God *created*.

The Hebrew word is *bara*, which means "shape, form, fashion, or create." It has a dynamic energy that is fluid and Spirit-breathed. Just like our Creator God, the word sparks the idea of boundless options and possibilities.

Since we are created in God's own image, we possess some of this creative energy too. Is it any wonder that when we are worn out, our creativity is often one of the first things to suffer?

Often when I am running low on energy, I find myself creating less and consuming more. Less making, less writing, less innovating; more consuming TV shows, goods, and food.

But what a shame when we allow weariness

to steal the God-given creativity in our souls by
mindlessly zoning out!

Maybe you don't think of yourself as creative;
but you're made in God's image, so you absolutely
are. Creativity can be conveyed through music
or art or numbers or data or words or ideas or
designs or something else entirely.

The truth is that it doesn't really matter what
form of expression it takes, just as long as you
use what God's put within you. Use it to bring
joy to his heart, because that's what you were
created for.

∾ Pause and Sift ∾

*Challenge yourself to do one small creative act every
day. Make an ethnic meal, rearrange a room in your
home, initiate imaginative play with your kids, or
fuel your curiosity by learning something new.*

Lord, I simply invite you to come and inspire
me afresh today. Would you breathe your
life and creativity into my weary soul?

ᏩGet Back Up

When people fall down, don't they get up again? When they discover they're on the wrong road, don't they turn back?

JEREMIAH 8:4

Have you ever avoided doing something because you were worried about failing?

Maybe you didn't apply for a job you wanted because you convinced yourself that the competition was too fierce. Perhaps you didn't share your opinions because you didn't want to be judged. Or possibly you didn't try out that new idea for fear it would flop.

The fear of failure affects everyone sometimes—even the most seemingly confident people. But many entrepreneurs will tell you that failure is not necessarily the opposite of success; rather, it's a prerequisite.

A common motto in Silicon Valley, where nine out of ten new tech start-ups fail, is "fail fast, fail often." In other words, failure can actually be a "win" if you can learn to use it to improve your plans and ideas.

Did you know that James Dyson went through 5,127 prototypes before he successfully launched the world's first bagless vacuum cleaner? Or that Henry Ford closed two failed car companies before launching the world's first mass-produced car?

So maybe instead of fearing failure, we should learn to reframe it as an opportunity to learn and grow.

It really doesn't matter how many times you fall flat on your face; it only matters that you get back up again when you do. Besides, surely the biggest failure of all is the failure to even try to step out and make your contribution to the world.

∽ Pause and Sift ∽

Consider what you would do if you knew there was no risk of failing. Now go and do it.

Lord, I'm sorry that I often let my fear of failure hold me back. Help me to get over my pride and self-protection and step out confidently in whatever you ask me to do.

Sharpen Your Attentiveness

*Be still in the presence of the LORD, and
wait patiently for him to act.*

PSALM 37:7

Do you often find yourself struggling to give anyone your undivided attention because an alert is
flashing on your phone screen? You pick up your
phone to read a message, only to end up being
pulled into another completely unrelated task.
Suddenly fifteen minutes have passed by and
you've been completely sidetracked from what
you were doing.

It's astonishing how technology has reshaped
our habits over recent years, and most of it for
good. But with so much information at our finger-
tips being scanned and processed by our brains,
it's no wonder that we sometimes can't stay
focused.

With our attention constantly fragmented,
is it a surprise that we end up feeling mentally

drained without having been productive at all?
A scattered mind creates a scattered life.

The Bible invites us to be still and wait
patiently for the Lord, to stop the constant
streams of information that often leave our brains
firing in so many directions.

If we want more clarity of mind, maybe we
need to silence the buzz of devices more often
and quietly make room for God's presence.

∽ Pause and Sift ∽

*Do a digital detox, but start small. Try unplugging for
an evening and create some focused time with God. Turn
off the TV, put devices away, and change your phone
setting to airplane mode. Consider doing this regularly.*

Lord, I know my mind often seems to race from one
thing to another, and I never seem to get anything done
that really matters. Help me to be more disciplined
in my focus and to direct my attention on you.

Remember Again

Let all that I am praise the Lord; may I never
forget the good things he does for me.

PSALM 103:2

It's really easy to become so preoccupied with each day's myriad different concerns that we forget about the goodness of God. But today's psalm calls us to keep remembering. When we do, our hearts are filled with thankfulness and praise.

But what about those times when life doesn't look like you thought it would, or when you can't see any of God's goodness?

I'm learning this is exactly when I need to remember him the most. Even when I can muster up only the tiniest bit of thankfulness in my heart, that momentary decision has the power to lift my spirit, change my perspective, and completely turn my day around.

Maybe that's why, for centuries, people have built temples, churches, and cathedrals in his name and filled them with beautiful, ornate works of art—to help them remember God's beauty. His glory. His goodness.

As impressive as these places are, we also need to build spaces for reflection in our own lives. Praise isn't something confined to a physical church building. The simple act of remembering enables us—his children—to enter into his courts at any time and in any place.

Let's stand out as people who don't hesitate to proclaim who our God is and everything he has done for us.

～ Pause and Sift ～

Ask God to make his goodness visible to you in the ordinary moments of your day. Write down what you see or snap a picture to remind you that this happens often.

Lord, help me be quick to remember all
your goodness to me and to encourage
others to do the same.

A Restful Life

Come to me, all of you who are weary and carry
heavy burdens, and I will give you rest.

MATTHEW 11:28

I recently enjoyed an overnight spa break with a
few girlfriends. It was just what we craved—a rare
chance to get away from work, parenting responsibilities, and the endless demands of everyday
life. I came away relaxed and recharged.

And though few of us have the time or money
for a luxurious getaway every time we need a
boost, the truth is that true rest was never meant
to be found only in a spa day or a week's vacation
in the sun.

As refreshing as those opportunities sound,
it's actually possible to find deep soul rest without
having to check out of normal life. Jesus invites us
to permanently live in his rest exactly where we
are. All we need to do is simply come to him.

Why not try it today? Don't leave your weariness on the couch or lay all your burdens in front
of the TV. You'll only pick them right back up

again. Instead, choose to bring them into his presence and experience his rest.

I know it can feel like a big effort when you're already tired and just want to switch off, but isn't it worth it to break free from your tiredness and anxiety? Who knows—maybe it will leave you feeling as refreshed as if you'd just stepped out of a spa.

∾ Pause and Sift ∾

Think of ways to actively enter into God's rest today. Play worship music as you work, or go for a short walk and pray during a break.

Lord, today I simply choose to live more freely in your presence by coming to you in my weariness and asking you to be my place of rest.

Be Thankful

*Be thankful in all circumstances, for this is God's
will for you who belong to Christ Jesus.*

1 THESSALONIANS 5:18

Some days it's fairly easy to feel thankful. But
what about those other days—days when it's
rainy and gray, when the kids are ill, or when you
haven't slept?

What about those days vexed with a broken
washing machine, a leaking bathroom pipe, or a
flat tire on the car?

On those sort of days, it doesn't usually feel
like there's much to be thankful for, does it?

And yet when I really stop and think, that's
simply not true. I am blessed in so many ways. In
fact, once I begin recalling all the things I have to
be grateful for, the list goes on and on.

Maybe that's why the Bible encourages us to
bring our thanksgiving before God more often
than it encourages us to present our needs.

God isn't insecure or egotistical. And he
doesn't really need our thanks and praise. But

maybe he knows that we need to offer thanks and praise in all circumstances for our own sake.

It's not about fake positivity, denying your feelings, or pretending that everything is perfect; it's about a change in your heart's attitude and your focus.

Thankfulness is so good for us: It lifts our spirits. It changes our perspectives. And it can literally turn a bad day into one in which we don't dwell on our problems but see God's goodness instead.

∾ Pause and Sift ∾

Write down everything you're thankful for. You'll be surprised at how many things there are. Just keep writing and let it inspire you.

Lord, thank you for blessing me in countless ways. Help me not to take your goodness for granted but to practice thankfulness every day, regardless of how I feel.

Love Yourself

I praise you because I am fearfully and wonderfully made.

PSALM 139:14, NIV

Isn't it ironic that in the age of the selfie so many people are plagued by feelings of low self-esteem?

A recent global study by Dove, a manufacturer of beauty products, surveyed women from thirteen developed countries and found that the majority surveyed were self-conscious about their appearance. Many respondents admitted they opted out of important life events because they didn't like the way they looked.

I find it incredibly sad that women feel pressured to conform to society's made-up ideas about what beauty is, so much so that they are actually choosing not to show up for their own lives.

Yet to be honest, I can be self-critical at times too. My postpregnancy body is more stretched out than it has ever been before. When I glance in the mirror, my face has more wrinkles, my hair is greyer, and I'm carrying a little extra weight. I wonder, *Where did the younger, slimmer, sexier version of me go?*

But the Bible reminds us that we are all fearfully and wonderfully made by God. Every human body is a complex design, incorporating several systems made up of innumerable intricate parts that keep us functioning from head to toe.

We are all living, breathing miracles—both inside and out—who are beautiful in God's eyes.

∾ Pause and Sift ∾

Pamper yourself this week. Make an appointment for a massage, get your nails done, or try a class that you've always wanted to join. Think of it as an act of self-love.

Lord, I'm sorry for the times I've been
critical of how I look. Would you help me
see myself through your eyes and practice
loving myself just as you love me?

Pursue Purpose

Don't wear yourself out trying to get rich.
Be wise enough to know when to quit.

PROVERBS 23:4

We live in an age when what you buy has become synonymous with who you are. And it seems like everyone is caught up in the chase for bigger, faster, better, smarter stuff.

But the truth is that God hasn't called us to pursue continuous lifestyle enhancement or increased personal affluence. Aspiration isn't a bad thing, but it's not the only thing. And it shouldn't be everything.

It's so easy to allow our life choices to be shaped by cultural expectations, values, or norms that focus on superficial markers of success, such as what you do or how much you earn, instead of who you are actually becoming.

I want a life anchored in contentment, not dissatisfaction; one marked by gratitude, not comparison.

But this sometimes means making brave

choices that go against the grain—like my recent decision not to apply for a promotion at work even though it offered financial benefits. Deep down, I knew it would stretch me too thin and prevent me from giving my best to my young family.

I'm not saying it's a decision I would make in every season of life, or that anyone else should do the same. Just don't be swept up by social norms without ever questioning them.

If you're after a life that really matters, don't wear yourself out chasing wealth. Start pursuing things with eternal purpose instead.

∽ Pause and Sift ∽

Spend a few moments considering the values shaping your life. Do you need to make any changes or adjustments?

Lord, I don't want to become so immersed in this consumer culture that I end up blending in. Help me to develop greater gratitude, contentment, and awareness of what you want for me.

Notice the Good

God looked over all he had made, and
he saw that it was very good!

GENESIS 1:31

My son just learned his numbers at school, so
he has begun counting stars from his bedroom
window before he goes to sleep. I enjoy watching
his delight. Did you know there are 9,096 stars in
the night sky visible from the earth? That's a lot of
stars to count before bedtime!

How wonderfully extravagant God's handi-
work is, and how intricately detailed in its design!
Yet how much of this beauty do we really notice
when we're rushing busily through our days?

In the story of Creation in Genesis, we read
how God took the time to pause and notice how
everything he made "was very good." In fact,
before this verse, the phrase "it was good" is
repeated six other times. God delighted in all
he had made. Isn't this also a clue about how he
intends for us to interact with his world?

The average person in the United States

spends 93 percent of their time enclosed in either buildings or vehicles, but there's something so regenerative about getting away from artificial lights and screens and retreating outdoors into the sunlight and fresh air.

You don't need to go far to feel the benefits either. Even if you live in a city, as I do, I'm sure you'll find plenty of beauty to appreciate right outside your front door.

∾ Pause and Sift ∾

Go for a short walk outside. Maintain a slow pace in order to see the beauty that's all around you, even in the most unexpected places.

Lord, so often I move through life
at such a rushed pace that I simply don't
pause to notice the natural beauty around me.
Today I am choosing to slow down and see
the goodness in all that you have made.

Troubleshoot Problems

*God is our refuge and strength, always
ready to help in times of trouble.*

PSALM 46:1

All of us experience troubles of varying degrees
at different times in our lives. They can range
from a devastating, life-changing situation to an
everyday problem such as a sick child, niggling
back pain, or a miscommunicated message.
When I experience the latter, I immediately think,
*I can't selfishly bother God with these small
inconveniences. They are too insignificant for
him. Far worse things happen to other people,
and he has bigger priorities. I need to pull myself
together and just get over it.*

But the truth is that as much as God cares
about the big issues in the world, my everyday
stresses and concerns matter to him as well.

He absolutely cares about the state of my
heart, my family, my health, and my home,

as well as the multitude of troubles that I read about each day in the news. He is big enough to handle it all!

God is always ready to help us, but maybe he is just waiting for us to ask. Slowly but surely I am learning how to let God be my refuge, my strength, and my help in times of trouble—whether serious or minor—just as he promised he would.

∿ Pause and Sift ∿

This week, stop and ask God for help every time you feel stressed out or under pressure or are struggling to cope with a problem.

Lord, I'm sorry that I don't always see you as the first solution to my problems. Help me to be humble enough to recognize my need and quicker to invite you to be my help.

Wait Well

Hope deferred makes the heart sick, but
a dream fulfilled is a tree of life.

PROVERBS 13:12

I don't know about you, but I really hate waiting.
And I'm really bad at it too.

In fact, I think I've complained my way
through every extended delay I've ever had to face
in my life.

I get frustrated when things don't seem to be
happening, but slowly I'm learning that sometimes waiting is necessary and even beneficial—
because when we're forced to linger longer than
anticipated, truly important things can happen.

It's easy to become disappointed when what
you hope for most has been deferred. At times
we can find ourselves wanting to scream out in
frustration, "God, why aren't you answering my
prayers?"

But whenever we start questioning God's
character, an infection begins to take root in our

hearts. I have been there more than once. Trust me—it isn't healthy.

Maybe instead of just praying for things to happen faster, a better approach might be to ask God what he wants to teach us through the waiting process. What lesson does he want to impress on our hearts? What personal qualities does he want to strengthen in us?

He might just send us little encouragements along the way, saying, "I love you and I haven't forgotten you. Something good is coming. Just wait and see."

So if you're waiting right now, try to remain patient! And ask God to work in your heart as you do.

∾ Pause and Sift ∾

If you're in a season of waiting, ask God to reveal what he wants to show you or teach you during this time.

Lord, you know my longings and the frustrations that I feel. Strengthen my resolve to wait well. Give me a soft and teachable heart as I continue to trust in you.

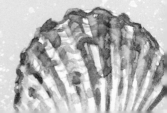

Feeling Invisible?

If you are faithful in little things, you
will be faithful in large ones.

LUKE 16:10

Do you ever feel like your hard work goes
unnoticed or that your efforts are overlooked?

My younger self had some pretty big dreams.
I wanted to change the world in a million different
ways. But these days I find myself sorting piles
of laundry and picking up LEGOs, wondering
whether my life is enough.

Still I continue on, even when it's boring or
when I'm exhausted, because deep down it matters to a little person who is depending on me.

Maybe your faithfulness doesn't look the
same as mine. Maybe you're faithful in a job or
a ministry where you feel underappreciated, or
in a friendship where you keep on giving but the
favors only seem to flow in one direction.

I love today's verse because it reminds me that
even on the hardest, most thankless or mundane
days, being faithful matters to God.

Life isn't really about those big success moments that happen on a large platform; it's about those small, seemingly unimportant moments that no one really notices, where you just keep showing up and giving it your best anyway.

Faithfulness is not a highly rated quality in our society. But keep going, keep turning up, keep giving life your all, and remember that the One we serve doesn't miss a thing. In due time, he promises to reward all those who are faithful to him.

∽ Pause and Sift ∽

Have you felt discouraged or tempted to quit recently? Spend some time in prayer today recommitting yourself to serving wherever God has placed you right now.

Lord, help me to be faithful with whatever you put in front of me today, trusting in you as I continue to serve an audience of one.

Lean into Joy

Always be full of joy in the Lord. I say it again—rejoice!
PHILIPPIANS 4:4

Life can offer us the most incredible highs, yet at other times life can be tinged with so much pain. But more often than not, our experience is somewhere in the middle, hovering between the mediocre and mundane. I think that's why the Bible so often reminds us to lean into joy.

It took me an embarrassingly long time to realize that sometimes the most spiritual thing you can do in life is to just lighten up a bit.

Even now, when I'm under pressure, I tell myself I'm too hurried and stressed for moments of joy; that I don't have time to laugh with colleagues or to be silly with my son.

Sometimes pursuing joy can seem a little bit self-indulgent. Shouldn't we be doing something more spiritual or useful instead?

But the truth is that not everything in life needs to be serious; there is purpose in having fun too. Enjoying life is not pointless, frivolous, or a waste of time, because it feeds our souls, it blesses others around us, and it brings joy to our Maker's heart.

Anything less than approaching life joyfully is just going through the motions; it's like settling for the black-and-white version of life when you could be enjoying a much richer experience with Ultra HD and enhanced surround sound.

So why not grab every opportunity to celebrate goodness, to embrace silliness, and to enjoy the fun side of life!

∾ Pause and Sift ∾

Do something that has absolutely no purpose, other than just being fun. Consider it a celebration of life and an act of worship to God.

Lord, I don't always see the value of
joy or recognize its spiritual worth.
Please show me opportunities to lean into joy.
May it be something I pursue each day.

Declutter Your Life

*Wherever your treasure is, there the
desires of your heart will also be.*

MATTHEW 6:21

Minimalism has surged in popularity recently,
thanks to the endless advice of style gurus, tips
from home-makeover shows, and strategies
in bestselling books—all teaching us how to
declutter our lives.

I have to admit that there's nothing I love
more than tidying up, purging closets, rearrang-
ing things, clearing surfaces, and creating new
space-saving solutions in my home. There's something so satisfying and freeing about getting rid
of unnecessary clutter and choosing to live with
less.

But for me, the idea of paring down possessions in a world where it's so easy to accumu-
late more goes far beyond the mere aesthetic
of a picture-perfect home, or even the practical
benefits of simplifying or streamlining my life.
It is also a spiritual practice.

When you have more, you worry more. I don't know about you, but I don't want to become so weighed down, tied up, or distracted by material things that I risk missing anything God has for me.

So my basic rule is that if I haven't used or worn something in the past year, then chances are I probably never will. It's time to give it to someone who needs it more. An uncluttered home helps keep my heart uncluttered too.

∽ Pause and Sift ∽

Be serious about decluttering. Get rid of things you have been holding on to but no longer need. Take your items to a resale shop or give them to someone who might need them more.

Lord, rather than hoarding my possessions or storing up my belongings for a rainy day that may never come, help me use them to bless someone else's life today. Would you teach me to hold things lightly, remembering that everything I have is yours?

Embrace Imperfection

My grace is all you need. My power works best in weakness.
2 CORINTHIANS 12:9

It's easy to look at someone's life and think it's more perfect than yours, especially through the lens of social media.

Deep down we all know that our Instagram and Facebook feeds don't reflect reality; they edit, enhance, filter, distort, and subtly spin the truth.

Are the people who post their remarks sincerely trying to brighten our day, or is it a form of self-gratification?

Yet how often do we still look at these glimpses of others' lives and instantly judge that they are happier, healthier, more popular, or more together than us?

As we evaluate ourselves in the midst of this continuous stream of heavily altered reality, we can also become our own worst critics by holding ourselves up to unrealistically high expectations.

These unattainable standards and images of flawlessness convince us that we don't measure up. And all too often we let the pursuit of perfection control us.

The truth is that following Jesus has simply never been about trying to be more perfect; it's about allowing his perfect sacrifice to cover all our imperfections.

Today's verse is a great reminder that there is actually beauty in imperfection and strength in weakness—because it's only when we admit our weakness before God that we get to experience more of his grace.

And when we admit our weaknesses to others, his power at work within us can really be seen.

∽ Pause and Sift ∽

Be honest about one of your flaws or weaknesses with someone—perhaps your partner, colleague, or kids—and see what grace unfolds when you do.

Lord, I'm sorry that I often get caught up in the pursuit of perfection. Help me to be quicker to admit my weaknesses and better at asking for your grace.

Cut the Complaining

Do everything without complaining and arguing.

PHILIPPIANS 2:14

Research shows that on average, most of us complain about once a minute during conversation. That's pretty staggering!

I really don't feel like I complain that often. But maybe complaining has become so normalized in our Western culture that we barely even notice it.

The Bible illustrates that habitual complaining has long been a part of human history. The Israelites continually grumbled to Moses about their hardships in the wilderness, despite God's supernatural provision for them.

He had sent them water from a rock, manna from heaven, quail that had been flying nearby, a pillar of fire to guide them by night, and a cloud to lead them by day. He had even parted a sea to deliver them from an enemy army. But still they ungratefully carried on.

That's the problem with complaining: It's incredibly contagious and easily reinforced. In fact, experts will tell you that repeated exposure to negative talk, whether it's yours or someone else's, actually begins to shrink your brain and rewire it toward a greater tendency to complain.

What's more, when you complain, your body releases a stress hormone called cortisol, which raises your blood pressure and makes you more susceptible to other risky health conditions. So when the Bible implores us to do everything without arguing or complaining, it really is sound advice!

Complaining can be a difficult habit to break, but the single best antidote I have ever found is proactively cultivating an attitude of gratitude for God's goodness instead.

∾ Pause and Sift ∾

Each time you feel a complaint stirring up inside, shift your attention to something you are grateful to God for instead.

Lord, I know I'm often guilty of complaining, arguing, and being too quick to forget your goodness. Would you help me to choose positivity over negativity and gratitude over complaining?

Learn to Linger

He began to cry out, "Son of David, Jesus!
Mercy, have mercy on me!" . . . Jesus stopped
in his tracks. "Call him over."

MARK 10:47, 49, MSG

When you're a doer like me, the urge to keep
racing to the next task can be hard to manage.
But recently, I've been trying to linger more.

That often means deciding to savor a sense
of achievement for a few moments before diving
headfirst into another task. I'm learning to appreciate the beauty of what's completed rather than
seeing only those things that are waiting to be
done.

I'm also learning to linger by intentionally
slowing down enough to really see each person
in front of me rather than just going through the
motion of a conversation. And maybe this is the
most important lingering of all.

Jesus regularly spent time with people, even
when he was in great demand. In fact, throughout
the Gospels we repeatedly see moments where

he was willing to be inconvenienced and linger long enough to participate in what his Father was doing.

Jesus took time to linger and converse with a Samaritan woman at a well; time to befriend and eat with corrupt tax collectors; time to listen to and answer the questions of a rich young ruler; and time to stop and heal a blind beggar on the roadside, as today's passage describes.

Jesus made time for all sorts of interruptions. If he needed time to reflect, to regroup, or to respond to someone else's need, shouldn't we be open to it too?

∾ Pause and Sift ∾

Try punctuating your day with small moments of lingering. Take short breaks between each task to simply pause, reflect, listen for God's voice, and notice and celebrate each small win.

Lord, I frequently rush to the next thing without really savoring or appreciating the moment I am in. Would you teach me how to linger longer?

Keep Calm

The LORD himself will fight for you. Just stay calm.

EXODUS 14:14

Have you ever been wrongly accused of something or felt unfairly attacked? How well did you handle it?

I've spent many years working in public relations and marketing, so handling criticism and defending my clients' reputation is fairly comfortable ground for me. And I'm pretty good at it too.

For as long as I can remember, I have always been able to easily influence, debate, and persuade. I've been told many times that I can literally argue that black is white.

However, my husband is the polar opposite; he really hates conflict of any kind. In fact, he would go to almost any length to keep the peace and avoid a disagreement, which makes for an interesting marriage dynamic at times!

Almost everyone naturally falls into a fight-or-flight response whenever they feel under attack—either defending themselves vehemently or fleeing from the perceived threat. In today's verse, Moses assures the Israelites who are fleeing from Egypt that God will protect them, even though Pharoah's army has caught up with them.

This reminds me there is another way of reacting under pressure, and that sometimes the best response is actually to just stay calm: not rushing into battle, and not running away either, but simply choosing to rest in God and allow him to be the One who fights on your behalf.

∽ Pause and Sift ∽

Next time you feel cornered, criticized, attacked, or misunderstood, take a deep breath, count to ten, and invite God right into that moment. Stay calm and rest in him.

Lord, help me to lay down my defensiveness and self-protection when I feel vulnerable. Help me to resist the urge to always leap to my own defense and instead trust you to fight for me.

Prioritize People

Do not forsake your friend or a friend of your family.
PROVERBS 27:10, NIV

It's so easy to let your everyday routine swallow you up whole. And often when we get too busy, we tend to take for granted the people who mean the most to us. But if you're anything like me, one day you will look up after a season of busyness and wonder where all your closest people went!

We allow overfamiliarity to prevent us from giving our best to family members who live under the same roof, or we allow exhaustion to stop us from connecting with friends nearby or far away.

I'm not very good at regularly keeping in touch or planning ahead to schedule catch-ups. Often I find I'm too overloaded in my here and now to even think about these things. It's never my intention to let my relationships slip or to treat people I care about like a low priority, but there are always just too many other things pressing on my time.

Then suddenly I realize that days have turned into weeks, and before I know it, entire months

142

have passed by and I haven't called, met up, or been in touch.

But the truth is that some relationships are simply too important to be relegated to the Christmas card list. These days I'm trying to make more of an effort to stay connected to people I love. Whenever I do, I discover that it is always, always worth it.

∾ Pause and Sift ∾

Either decide to reconnect with a far-off friend or family member this week or do something to make yourself more present and available for those you live with.

Lord, thank you for the huge blessing of friends and family in my life. Help me to plan my time and prioritize my people better, that I might invest in those who matter the most to me.

Quit Future-Tripping

*How do you know what your life will be like
tomorrow? Your life is like the morning fog—
it's here a little while, then it's gone.*

JAMES 4:14

Some of us have the exhausting habit of "future-tripping"—mentally obsessing about the future, often at the expense of our present.

It's as if we have learned to rest all our hopes and dreams on the achievement of some yet-to-come idealistic state of being: marriage, parenthood, a promotion, or even retirement.

So we work, save, plan, and strategize to achieve these perfect conditions of happiness that are somewhere in our imagined future. Yet sometimes we end up shouldering unnecessary stress by worrying about how to get the future we want instead of enjoying the present we already have.

I don't know what the future you're envisioning looks like, but what if your version doesn't actually match up with God's? Or worse still, what if you do eventually achieve all those predetermined conditions of happiness, only to find out they still leave you unsatisfied?

The truth is that future-tripping is probably the world's greatest con. If you can't be happy right now, chances are you probably won't be happy then either.

It's not a bad thing to have a clear vision for your future; just don't live there or let it over-shadow your present. Don't miss the life that God has for you now.

∾ Pause and Sift ∾

Instead of worrying about things to come, start the daily practice of noticing—and writing down—three things you are grateful for in your present.

Lord, I don't want to risk overlooking anything that you have for me today. Would you please help me to be more centered in the present?

Pace Yourself

Slow down. Take a deep breath. What's the hurry?
Why wear yourself out? Just what are you after anyway?

JEREMIAH 2:25, MSG

I love getting ready for a vacation: the packing and preparation, the excitement and anticipation, the promise of warmer climates and new places to explore.

But most of all, I love that sweet sense of relief in leaving work and other responsibilities behind, if only for a few days.

Like me, do you crash and burn more than you'd like to admit? Today's verse reminds us that God doesn't take pleasure in our working ourselves into the ground for fifty weeks, only to collapse in sheer exhaustion for two.

In his prophetic words through Jeremiah, God warns us to check our motivations: to ask ourselves some honest questions about what we're really working so hard for, and what we believe about God in the process. If we're not careful, we can become more distanced from him.

If your life often seems hectic or overly burden-some, maybe it's time to consider reordering your priorities and pacing yourself more. Since we tend to plan everything in our lives, why not consider rest as an activity in your schedule too?

Once you begin to incorporate it as part of your normal life rhythm, you will feel more refreshed, and it will make your planned vacation time less an act of desperation and more fully a time of enjoyment.

～ Pause and Sift ～

What brings you rest? How can you include it in the daily or weekly rhythm of your life? Schedule that rest time in!

Lord, I want to maintain a healthy work-rest balance and to be motivated by the right things. Would you give me the wisdom to pace myself by developing healthy rhythms of work and rest?

Overcome Self-Doubt

Let God transform you into a new person
by changing the way you think.

ROMANS 12:2

How loud is the voice of shame or self-doubt in your life? That unspoken fear of not being good enough or lacking what it takes to succeed can be a huge challenge for many people in our success-oriented world—especially for women.

For example, research has shown that women are far less likely to apply for work promotions than their male counterparts, even when they are equally qualified. One major corporation found that men felt confident applying for a job when they met 60 percent of the criteria, whereas most women applied only if they felt they met 100 percent of the requirements.

Although caution isn't always a bad thing, it's unfortunate when women allow perfectionism, feelings of shame, low self-esteem, or the fear of failure to hold them back from stepping out and trying new things.

I often wonder how many more female leaders there might be in our communities, businesses, churches, or schools if women really felt empowered—and how much richer might our society be as a result.

It's possible to feel shame and inadequacy about so many different things: our body image, age, or mental health; our parenting, families, and homes.

But the gospel assures us that we don't need to live under the weight of shame. God's perfect love drives out all our fear, and we are freed to pursue our calling with him.

∾ Pause and Sift ∾

Are there any areas in your life hampered by shame or self-doubt? Ask God to show you how he sees you today, and begin to believe it.

Lord, I want your voice of love and affirmation to be the loudest voice in my life—louder than the voice of my own shame, fear, or self-doubt.

Pay More Attention

He must become greater; I must become less.

JOHN 3:30, NIV

So much of the current cultural climate is about
feeding an individual's need for attention. Just
look at the increased number of social media
influencers, reality TV stars, and celebrities who
are revered just for being famous.

Isn't that desire for recognition within us all
to some degree? It's in every pang of jealousy we
experience when someone else gets promoted
and in each sense of affirmation we feel when
someone likes our social media posts.

Yet craving attention is so contrary to the
gospel of Jesus. He invites us to live with less ego,
less pride, and less selfish ambition in exchange
for more of his humility, loving-kindness, and
grace.

It sounds like such a simple trade-off, doesn't
it? Less of me for more of him. So why is it so
hard in practice?

The truth is that chasing after our own glory

and fame is the original sin that caused Satan to fall from heaven; he wanted to become more, to become his own god. That same power struggle has been plaguing humankind ever since.

What would happen if we chose to become people who paid attention instead of people who crave attention?

I really think it's the perfect antidote to our narcissistic culture. The simple act of devoting more attention to Jesus and the beauty he created that's all around us will take our eyes off ourselves and refocus our hearts on glorifying God.

∼ Pause and Sift ∼

Practice curiosity by paying more attention to what's around you. Let it inspire you and shift your gaze toward God.

Lord, I can be so self-absorbed and focused on boosting my own ego and reputation. Would you help me to take my eyes off myself and turn them onto you?

True Contentment

Don't love money; be satisfied with what you have. For God has said, "I will never fail you. I will never abandon you."

HEBREWS 13:5

Have you ever found yourself trying to buy your way to greater happiness? Me too. And it's usually when I've had a bad day.

Our consumer culture constantly tells us that if we don't feel good, there's a product we can buy to fill the void and fix the issue.

We can go online and shop for a revitalizing face cream, a hair-restoring product, a designer handbag, fancier shoes, the latest gadget, a kitchen renovation, a bigger car, or a family vacation. Our craving to consume can be fulfilled at any time and in any place—with one click of a button.

The problem with constant consumption is that it never actually delivers on its promises. It follows the law of diminishing returns. In fact, most studies show that even where income and spending increase significantly, there is absolutely no correlating increase in happiness at all.

I desperately want a life that's anchored in contentment rather than feeling weighed down by a nagging sense of dissatisfaction and longing for more.

Today's verse helps me recenter my life on the truth that true contentment can't be discovered through amassing more things; it's found by being at peace with what I already have.

The priceless treasure we can all have is God's unending presence with us and his commitment to never fail or abandon us.

∽ Pause and Sift ∾

Do you sometimes struggle with contentment? Spend some time meditating on today's verse and thanking God for his presence with you.

Lord, thank you for being here with me now. I want to find my contentment in you, not in things I buy. You are everything I need. Help me to embrace that truth.

When the Unexpected Happens

We stopped relying on ourselves and
learned to rely only on God.

2 CORINTHIANS 1:9

It's easy to fool yourself into thinking that you're trusting God when everything is going your way; but it's much harder when the unexpected suddenly interrupts your life.

It can turn up in many different ways and times: an unplanned bill for a major house repair, a relationship breakup, or a diagnosis of ill health, to name a few.

Whenever it happens, we're caught completely off guard and often left feeling underprepared, overwhelmed, and out of control.

But why are we so often surprised by the unexpected? The Bible actually warns us to be ready for all kinds of trials and challenges in life. And why do we allow them to unsettle us so easily when the Bible encourages us to see our difficulties as opportunities for growth?

What if we could actually reframe our fear of the unexpected and learn to see life's biggest interruptions as chances to stop relying on ourselves and discover a deeper dependence on God instead? Perhaps they would lose their power to paralyze us.

I know this is easy to talk about but a whole lot harder to do. So how do you actually learn to rely on God when disruptions invade your life, and how do you prevent these situations from stealing your peace?

Maybe if we practice relying on God more fully in the everyday interruptions, we'll find it easier to depend on him when crisis hits our lives.

∽ Pause and Sift ∾

As you experience small disruptions, inconveniences last-minute changes, or even a major crisis this week, ask yourself, Is God trying to get my attention and giving me an opportunity to practice relying on him?

_____

Lord, help me to approach every unexpected situation, however small or large, as an opportunity to deepen my reliance on you.

Recover Your Life

Are you tired? Worn out? Burned out on religion?
Come to me. Get away with me and you'll recover
your life. I'll show you how to take a real rest.
Walk with me and work with me—watch how
I do it. Learn the unforced rhythms of grace.

MATTHEW 11:28-29, MSG

For quite a long time, my life resembled semi-organized chaos rather than following any real spiritual rhythms, let alone any "unforced rhythms of grace."

But lately my husband and I have been exploring how we can introduce more authentic spiritual rhythms into our everyday lives—without just cramming in more activity. One change I've made is to listen to Scripture on audio and pray while I'm commuting to work.

I really love today's verses because they remind me that faith was never meant to be full of must-dos or ought-tos.

Jesus came to offer us relationship, not religion, and all those self-imposed expectations and rules that we place on ourselves are exactly what he came to free us from.

Whenever I feel that following Jesus is a heavy burden, I reread this passage and check my heart's motivation.

I want to develop new ways of expressing my faith that feel less like rhythms of unsustainable self-effort and more like simple, "unforced rhythms of grace."

Jesus invites each of us to find real rest in his presence; to watch how he does it and follow his lead.

～ Pause and Sift ～

Consider some simple daily or weekly spiritual rhythms you could introduce into your life that would feel life-giving and help you to rest in God.

Lord, I don't want religion; I want a relationship with you. Help me to identify anything that I might need to put down or take up in order to grow closer to you.

Shrink Problems,
Enlarge God

*O magnify the LORD with me, and let
us exalt his name together.*

PSALM 34:3, KJV

I don't know about you, but whenever something
goes wrong, my mind often jumps to the worst-
case scenario. If anyone tries to assure me that
things will work out, I mentally dismiss them.
And I find it hard to relax until the problem is
taken care of.

One of the issues with this type of thinking is
that lots of dilemmas can't be solved immediately.
Some solutions take time to unfold and require
patience.

All our worrying, obsessing, and feeling
defeated by the size of a problem rarely changes
our circumstances. In fact, overfocusing on a
predicament only makes it seem larger and more
insurmountable, dashing any bit of resolve we may
have mustered to continue seeking an answer.

Maybe that's why the psalmist David calls us to "magnify the LORD." To magnify God literally means to make him larger and give him more focus in our lives. That's what happens each time we begin to worship him.

The decision to worship God doesn't necessarily mean he will provide an instant fix for all our problems. But it does change how we perceive them.

As our focus on God gets bigger, suddenly our worries seem so much smaller. And as our attention moves from our troubles to God's greatness, he gives us the courage and faith to overcome our obstacles.

∾ Pause and Sift ∾

Practice shrinking your problems by magnifying God. Spend some time reminding yourself of his greatness today; you could try memorizing Scripture verses to help you.

Lord, I recognize that I often tend to focus on my problems, only to end up feeling more overwhelmed. Help me shift my attention away from the issue and onto you today.

The Secret of Refreshment

The generous will prosper; those who refresh others will themselves be refreshed.

PROVERBS 11:25

I love the idea of hospitality, but usually when I say I would love to have people over more often, I follow it with a "but" or a "when."

"*But* my kitchen table is too small, my toddler is too wild, my house is too messy, and my time and energy are too stretched."

Or "*When* we have a bigger house with more space, my son is easier to manage, and my culinary skills improve" (which really means never!).

Yet I've discovered people will almost always say yes when I extend an invitation. They don't really pay attention to any of the things I'm obsessing over. They come to my home for friendship, laughter, and fun.

The same is true for you, too. Guests don't care whether you cook a meal from scratch or order pizza, whether they sit at a perfectly laid table or on the living room carpet.

No one is judging you for the laundry hanging over the chairs, the toys strewn across the floor, or yesterday's dishes left in the sink. They accept them as signs of a full life and a well-loved home.

Even though offering hospitality might sometimes feel like one more thing to do, prioritizing connection with others can lead to times of refreshment.

So don't default to *buts* and *whens*. And don't let the fear of things not being perfect prevent you from opening up your life. God will use whatever you have to bless someone else.

∾ Pause and Sift ∾

Make plans for hospitality this week. Invite someone to a playdate with the kids, a chat over coffee, or a meal with your family.

Lord, help me to choose hospitality as a lifestyle right now, not just one day "when" . . . even if things are imperfect.

When Is It Enough?

What do you benefit if you gain the whole
world but lose your own soul?

MARK 8:36

Our society is suffering from spiraling levels of consumption and personal debt, and it's easy to identify the cause.

Marketing experts estimate that we've gone from being exposed to about five hundred advertisements and marketing messages a day back in the 1970s to consuming around five thousand in 2006. And that number has certainly continued to increase.

Is it any wonder that so many of us are dis-contented? It's becoming harder to avoid the tsunami of marketing in public spaces, but we are also barraged in our homes and private conversa-tions via our personal devices.

Today's verse reminds me that if you are feel-ing isolated, exhausted, and spiritually empty, it doesn't matter how beautiful your home looks, how happy your family appears to others on social media, or how much cool stuff you own. Whatever represents gaining "the whole world" to you is utterly meaningless if it costs you your soul in the process. And as the apostle Matthew adds, "Is anything worth more than your soul?"

Don't buy into lies by spending every moment working so you can buy temporary things. And don't spend money as if you were trusting in material things to save you. Only God can save you.

Your soul is not expendable. There *is* a better way to live. Choose to lose the world and gain a healthy soul.

∾ Pause and Sift ∾

Clean out your in-box. Unsubscribe from unwanted marketing emails, cancel some subscriptions, and delete any mobile apps that continually spam you with distracting ads.

Lord, today I am choosing to pursue substance over style, connection with people over the accumulation of more stuff, and the well-being of my soul over material gain.

Avoid Spiritual Burnout

*Then Moses said, "If you don't personally go
with us, don't make us leave this place."*

EXODUS 33:15

Have you ever felt maxed out with Christian
activities? Maybe you lead worship, help with
kids' ministries, host a small group, attend prayer
meetings, volunteer for community outreach projects, and more.

It's perfectly possible to be doing all the right
things without being right on the inside at all.

Whenever I find myself talking about what I
should be doing or resenting the commitments
I've already made, it's a sure sign I'm operating
out of religious duty or obligation to others and
that it's probably time to cut back.

In contrast, have you ever experienced a time
when God's presence clearly showed up during
your spiritual service? How different was that
experience? How much more effortless did it feel?

When I first left home at eighteen to go to university, I remember praying, "God, I don't want empty religion. I want your presence to be real to me. And I want a faith that makes a difference in this world." Do you know what happened? God took me at my word and completely redirected my future plans.

It's been more than twenty years since I first uttered that sentiment, but it's still the litmus test for almost everything I do. Because if God's presence isn't with us, we are only busy being busy—just like everybody else.

This world doesn't need more busy or burned-out people; it needs people who carry the presence of God with them everywhere they go.

∿ Pause and Sift ∿

Consider stopping or cutting back on any commitments or activities in your life that feel lifeless, aren't bearing fruit, or are no longer nurturing your spiritual growth.

Lord, sometimes I get so caught up in well-meaning activities that I end up feeling resentful or burned out. Give me discernment to know what I should be involved in. I want everything I do to glorify you.

Humorous Relief

She is clothed with strength and dignity, and
she laughs without fear of the future.

PROVERBS 31:25

When was the last time you woke up, got out of
bed, and immediately wanted to crawl back under
the blankets because you didn't want to face the
day? You were exhausted and defeated before you
even left the bedroom.

Anxiety often starts with just a small, nagging
thought that creates more nagging thoughts. One
small worry overlays another, and before you
know it, you're panicking about something that
hasn't even happened and maybe never will.

I've heard it said that 10 percent of life is
about what happens to you, and 90 percent
is about how you respond. But even when we
know that stressing about things we can't influence or change is a waste of energy, we continue
worrying.

There are lots of different ways to practice
letting go of our worry, such as relaxation,

journaling, and mindfulness. But the relief you can get from laughing is really no joke.

In fact, laughter is one of the best medicines for worry. Did you know that when you laugh, it actually causes physical changes to your body that reduce anxiety and stress and boost your overall sense of well-being? How amazing is that!

Give it a try. Find something that's amusing, and let laughter begin to chase those worries away.

∾ Pause and Sift ∾

Do something that makes you laugh: Hang out with someone who has a great sense of humor, go see some (clean) stand-up comedy, read or watch something amusing, or just begin noticing the funny side of life more.

Lord, I want to feel inspired and excited about tomorrow, next week, and next month, not overwhelmed or full of dread. Would you teach me how to face the future with laughter?

Too Busy to Care?

*If someone has enough money to live well and
see a brother or sister in need but shows no
compassion—how can God's love be in that person?*

1 JOHN 3:17

Sometimes the immense brokenness in our
world can feel daunting amid our hectic lives,
can't it? Yet it's important to not let busyness
harden our hearts or cause us to switch off.

If you have money in a bank account, food
in your cupboards, a roof over your head, clean
water, clothes to wear, or access to education,
employment, and a car, then you have a lot—
certainly enough to share with others who
have less.

I know it can be hard to know where to begin
when the need around you feels so great, but
that's not an excuse for doing nothing. If we're
serious about following Jesus, we can't just
choose to ignore his words about defending the
poor, the weak, the orphans, and the widows.

It's a sentiment that I want to shape my life.

So these days I'm trying to live with open hands and an open heart in lots of simple, everyday ways. Will you join me?

If you're not sure where to start, begin right where you are. Befriend a lonely neighbor, buy coffee or a meal for someone who's homeless, or volunteer some time to a local project.

Never ever doubt that your small gestures of kindness can make a big difference in someone else's life as you seek to be Jesus' hands and feet wherever you are.

∾ Pause and Sift ∾

Ask God to show you one small, practical thing you can do to help someone else in your local community this week.

Lord, I know I'm often too busy to really notice or respond to the needs of others around me. But today, would you open my eyes and soften my heart?

Stay Focused

Let us strip off every weight that slows us down,
especially the sin that so easily trips us up. And let us
run with endurance the race God has set before us.

HEBREWS 12:1

Life seems to be an endless stack of priorities we are expected to balance: career, family, fitness, relationships, finances, spiritual life, and more. Each one demands our attention and competes for our time.

Sometimes we can fool ourselves into thinking that we're doing a pretty good job of juggling them all. But too often our anxiousness and irritability give us away.

So what are your priorities right now? If you don't know or you can't articulate them clearly, you will probably just end up running around in circles trying to keep all of those balls in the air. Sooner or later one of them is bound to drop.

It's much better to pick one or two priorities in each season of life and really concentrate on them, just like an athlete would do during training.

But perhaps more difficult than identifying your main priorities is deciding what you will give up in order to achieve them. Are there old habits or mindsets that you need to let go of, or unhelpful distractions that steal your time? Even good things can trip us up.

Don't allow a lack of focus to become your downfall. Refocus on the goal and strip off everything that hinders you. But most of all, fix your eyes on Jesus, who is our perfect example of how to run this race of life well.

∽ Pause and Sift ∽

What do you need to prioritize, and what do you need to let go of? Share your decisions with someone you trust and ask that person to keep you accountable.

Lord, give me clarity on what my priorities should be right now. Then help me run with single-minded focus and endurance toward my goal.

Hit Pause

Pay attention. . . . Stop and consider
the wonderful miracles of God!

JOB 37:14

We live in a culture that overvalues busyness,
don't we? Even busyness that doesn't make us
more productive.

We have 24-7 access to emails, shopping,
banking, dating, entertainment, and a never-
ending cycle of news—all of which can be great.
But hasn't it also become a bit of a burden?

It's like we've been conditioned to believe that
movement and motion are more desirable than
pausing—even when they don't really take us anywhere useful.

Often it can seem like being busy is the right
thing to do, but busyness without a clear purpose
can be worse than standing still.

You see this play out in workplaces all the
time. People hold meetings about meetings, and
nothing is actually accomplished. Not sure what
to do? Just do something. Look busy.

I guess sometimes it's easier to stay busy than to ask hard questions about whether things are working or how they could be better.

Think about hitting pause to reassess. Maybe pause and consider God.

When we do so, our perspective begins to shift, and it opens us up to new, creative ways of thinking and enables fresh faith to be released.

Isn't it worth practicing pausing in our lives, especially if it's pausing to consider God and what he might have to say?

∿ Pause and Sift ∿

If you are lacking clarity, press the pause button on activity for a moment. Stop and consider God today. Ask him for his guidance, and get busy listening to what he has to say.

Lord, I know there have been times I've believed that busyness is better than pausing. In this world that puts a high value on activity, would you give me the courage to pause and consider you?

Calm in a Crisis

When Jesus woke up, he rebuked the wind and said to the waves, "Silence! Be still!" Suddenly the wind stopped, and there was a great calm.

MARK 4:39

Do you ever feel battered by the winds of change or overwhelmed by waves of despair? When the storms of life hit, whether caused by sickness, overstretched finances, job uncertainty, relationship difficulties, or something else, they can leave you feeling incredibly vulnerable and out of control.

Anyone who has ever been caught in a real storm while out on the water understands the paralyzing terror the disciples felt as waves crashed into their boat. They panicked as the boat began to fill with water while Jesus, who was sleeping in the back, seemed unaffected.

Not surprisingly, the disciples woke him up, saying, "Teacher, don't you care that we're going to drown?" I find this detail in the story reassuring. When a crisis strikes, what is often our first reaction? We question God's care for us, just as the disciples did.

But Jesus' actions instantly put the disciples' doubt and fear to rest. He was perfectly in control, even when circumstances looked wildly chaotic. The storm immediately stilled at the sound of his voice.

Jesus is still in the business of calming storms in our lives today. When you know how committed he is to you, it is possible to be completely at peace, even in the midst of the tumult.

∽ Pause and Sift ∽

Are you anxious or fearful about anything? Find a quiet space and spend time meditating on the truth that Jesus is in control. Let it begin to calm your soul.

Lord, would you calm the storms swirling around my life right now, as well as those raging inside my heart?

Perspective Is Everything

The Lord isn't really being slow about
his promise, as some people think.
No, he is being patient for your sake.

2 PETER 3:9

I once heard someone say that if they could buy God anything, it would be a watch. I totally agree with this sentiment because often God's timing seems so much slower than I would like.

Waiting can be hard on our highly driven, impatient, human temperaments—especially when we're waiting for something we really want.

But time is a strange mix of reality and perception. When we focus on the delay, time seems to move more slowly. But often when we look back afterward, we realize that perhaps the wait wasn't so impossibly long after all.

To my four-year-old, a twenty-minute drive can feel never-ending, but as an adult, I consider it a short trip. And so it is with God. A human lifetime may seem long, but to God it's just a short, fleeting moment in the span of eternity.

So perhaps the real question we should be asking when we're waiting is not, "How much longer?" but rather, "Do I trust God, the author of time, to act at the very best time?"

Once you resolve this issue, you can focus on making the most of the waiting time instead of feeling frustrated.

As today's verse assures us, God is not slow in keeping his promises. But sometimes his timing only makes sense with the benefit of hindsight. Our responsibility in the middle is to trust him.

∾ Pause and Sift ∾

If you're waiting for something, ask yourself, What am I at risk of overlooking or missing out on right now that I won't have once the waiting is over?

Lord, thank you for being patient with me
in the midst of my fretting. Help me to
trust in your faithfulness even when I don't
fully understand what's going on.

Don't Give Up

Let's not get tired of doing what is good. At just the right time we will reap a harvest of blessing if we don't give up.

GALATIANS 6:9

I am not much of a finisher; I like the idea of starting something new more than the reality of actually doing it.

I have taken up many different hobbies over the years. And as a result, I'm a novice at snowboarding, skiing, surfing, tennis, beat mixing, cycling, jogging, salsa dancing, web design, and photography, just to name some of my fleeting interests.

The problem is that I don't want to be a beginner. I want to be good at everything right away. Unfortunately, I tend to get bored and frustrated, and then my interest begins to wane way before I master anything!

When it comes to hobbies, I accept the fact that I prefer dabbling—it's just how I'm wired. However, when it comes to loving God and others, I never want to get tired of doing good because it's such important work.

We may not see any tangible impact or change, which can be discouraging. But today's verse reminds us that in God's Kingdom, the effort is always worth it.

God promises that a season of reaping is coming. Maybe it's not today or even this year. Maybe we won't be the ones who actually see the harvest firsthand. But God is counting on us to keep spreading his message of hope.

∾ Pause and Sift ∾

Do one thing this week to help ignite or refuel your spiritual passion. Read a book, listen to a podcast, or attend an inspiring event that will motivate you.

Lord, sometimes I get tired of serving you when I can't see any return for my labor. Forgive my tendency to wonder, *What's in it for me?* Help me be faithful in all that you ask of me.

Keep It Simple

Jesus replied, "The most important commandment
is this: . . . 'You must love the LORD your God
with all your heart, all your soul, all your mind,
and all your strength.'" The second is equally
important: "Love your neighbor as yourself." No
other commandment is greater than these.

MARK 12:29-31

Sometimes we can make faith so complicated, can't we? And yet it really is so simple.

Jesus clearly said that loving God and loving others are the two guiding principles his followers should live by. Yet how often do we get caught up in one at the expense of neglecting the other?

I know there were times when I loved others with lots of activity, social action, and service. But while doing those things, I didn't spend much time in God's presence, and I soon burned out.

There were also times when my faith was all about me, centered on my own personal growth without any outlet for service. It became self-indulgent and lost its relevance.

That's why Jesus said that "no other commandment is greater than *these*." It's not either/or—it's both/and. Anything less is unbalanced.

It can be hard to strike the perfect balance. But Jesus gave us the ultimate example of how to do this well. He was both the Son of God and the friend of sinners. He often withdrew from crowds to be alone with his Father, but he also spent quality time connecting and ministering to people.

"God is love," and he commands us to live in his love. So let's love well, love big, and love deep.

∾ Pause and Sift ∾

Demonstrate your love for God and your neighbor in a practical way this week.

Lord, I want a life that's pleasing to you. Would you teach me how to love you and others well?

Activate Yourself

Do you not know that in a race all the
runners run, but only one gets the prize?
Run in such a way as to get the prize.

1 CORINTHIANS 9:24, NIV

Maybe it seems strange to read about running
in a book encouraging you to rest. But curiously
enough, getting regular exercise tends to leave us
feeling more energized and optimistic.

In fact, research indicates that just twenty
minutes of physical activity a day can significantly
improve your emotional and physical well-being.
Maybe if we really understood that greater personal happiness is just a light jog away, we might
all get on our feet a little bit more!

After putting it off for a long time, I've (slowly!)
been getting back into running again following
several years of relative inactivity during my pregnancies and new parenthood.

I can easily come up with excuses for avoiding
something that's challenging: *I'm too tired; I'm*
too busy; it's too dark after work, too wet in the

winter, too hot in the summer. But really, I just don't want to do it!

And yet I've discovered that getting fitter can be a spiritual pursuit too. Training your body physically can actually help you to develop greater mental strength, self-discipline, and perseverance in every area of life.

So find an activity you love. It doesn't really matter what it is; it just matters that you do it and that you commit to giving it your all—like any athlete in training would.

∾ Pause and Sift ∾

Make regular exercise a priority in your life. Sign up for a class, renew that fitness club membership, join a sports team, or try something new.

———————

Lord, I resolve to become a person of action, not just someone with good intentions. Give me the discipline to start today, not "perhaps one day."

When Life's Not Fair

His father said to him, "Look, dear son, you have
always stayed by me, and everything I have is yours."

LUKE 15:31

If you grew up in a Christian family or have spent
time in church, you are most likely familiar with
the story of the Prodigal Son. There are three
main characters—the wasteful younger brother;
the reliable older brother; and the gracious, loving
father. More often than I care to admit, I identify
with the older brother.

When you've always tried to faithfully do the
right things, it's really easy to end up resenting
those who make bad decisions but are given what
may seem like special treatment.

There have been numerous times when I've
found myself complaining, "It's not fair" because
someone less deserving—in my eyes at least—has
been more blessed than I have.

But isn't that the point? Nothing about grace is
fair. It was never meant to be. If any of us got what
was fair, we would all be separated from God.

It's easy to forget that the faithful brother was a sinner just as much as the Prodigal Son. His response to his father's elaborate display of grace only serves to highlight the true state of his heart. He essentially says, "But what about me?"

I love this story because it's so human. Haven't we all felt this way sometimes? But the father's response silences that sentiment once and for all: "Everything I have is yours." As a child of God, you share it all.

∿ Pause and Sift ∿

Thank God every single time you notice him bless someone else's life, whether in small or large ways.

Lord, I'm sorry that sometimes I focus on fairness rather than on your abundance of grace. Help me to be as quick to rejoice in your goodness toward others as I am when you bless my own life.

Experience His Comfort

The more we suffer for Christ, the more God will shower us with his comfort through Christ.

2 CORINTHIANS 1:5

I like comfort. To me, comfort is eating popcorn while I'm watching an old movie. It's sipping hot cocoa in front of a roaring fire on a cold, wintry day. It's taking a relaxing bath while surrounded by candles and music and curling up on the couch with a good book.

But today's verse describes true comfort from God's point of view.

Do you want to know "the God of all comfort" better? I think to myself, *Sure, that sounds nice . . .* until I realize that suffering is the prerequisite. *Hmmm, on second thought, I think I'll stick with chocolate and movies.* I'm joking, but only partially!

It can be tempting to think that being a Christian exempts us from suffering, or that our faith acts as some kind of FastPass to get us through pain. But the truth is that God never promised to give us an easy life; he promised to draw near to us in our suffering.

Although I wouldn't have chosen the heartbreak of pregnancy losses to be a part of my story over the past few years, I know that without those painful experiences there would be parts of God's character that I would never have discovered.

We follow a Savior who is acquainted with suffering far better than we are. He holds out his nail-pierced hands and asks us to follow him.

∽ Pause and Sift ∾

Do you need God's comfort right now? Or do you know someone who does? In what practical ways can you draw nearer to the God of all comfort or help someone else to experience his comfort today?

Lord, give me the courage to draw near to you in seasons of suffering. I want to know you more intimately and receive your comfort.

Stand Firm

Put on every piece of God's armor....
Stand your ground.
EPHESIANS 6:13-14

Have you been praying for a positive change in a situation, but the breakthrough just hasn't seemed to come? You have donned God's armor for protection against the enemy, but you've been battered by the fight and are battle weary, more than a little bit tempted to quit.

Perhaps you've even been in this exasperated place for so long that you've found yourself asking God, "What more can I possibly do?"

I have too. And do you know what? It's okay to feel that way. But just don't give up the fight!

Because when you've taken all the action that you can possibly take, said all the prayers that you can muster up, and declared all the truth that you can speak over a situation, what else is left?

The Bible says to keep standing firm.

Sometimes it can literally take everything within you to keep standing firm on the promises of God, can't it? But don't sit down, don't opt out, don't discard any piece of armor. Don't give up just yet. Choose to keep on standing. Remember, God is trustworthy and has already secured the victory.

Stand your ground by keeping your feet firmly planted on the promises of God until you overcome.

∼ Pause and Sift ∼

Are you feeling battle weary? Which promises of God do you need to recall and arm yourself with in order to keep standing firm today? Memorize them and keep speaking them over yourself.

Lord, I acknowledge that sometimes I have no more fight left inside me. Continue to be my strength as I choose to keep standing firm in you.

Invest in Friends

*Confess your sins to each other and pray for
each other so that you may be healed.*

JAMES 5:16

I love today's verse because it reminds me that
healing is most readily found within community,
through being in relationship with others.

That's why I'm part of a small group of close
girlfriends from my church that meets every
couple of weeks to catch up, share our hearts,
and pray for one another.

Over the years, we've been through so many
different ups and downs in life together: dating
and breakups, engagements and weddings,
becoming parents for the first time and losing
pregnancies, health problems, job changes,
divorce, and more.

Through all the celebrations and heartbreaks
that life has brought, we've laughed together,
cried together, prayed together, grown together,
and cheered one another on, standing in faith and

fighting in each friend's corner, even when we've not had the courage to battle for ourselves.

I am so grateful to God for these women he has put in my life. I can be real and vulnerable with them without any fear of judgment; I can access our WhatsApp group for advice or prayers at any time of the day or night and know they will always speak the truth to me.

Do you have friendships in your life with this kind of authenticity and accountability? There is such freedom, healing, and strength to be found in doing life alongside other women of God and pursuing your healing together.

∽ Pause and Sift ∽

This week, foster more openness and honesty in a friendship with another believer. Be vulnerable and share your struggles.

Lord, thank you for the blessing of authentic friendships in my life. Help me to pursue them, to invest in them, and to never take them for granted.

ʗhange Is
Here to Stay

*Every good and perfect gift is from above, coming
down from the Father of the heavenly lights,
who does not change like shifting shadows.*

JAMES 1:17, NIV

How is it that so many of us feel time-poor and
worn out, even though we have more leisure time
than any generation before us?

Maybe all those time-saving gadgets we fill
our lives with are just allowing us to squeeze
more and more into our ever-fuller days, or the
sheer amount of choices available to us actually
makes us waste more time overthinking simple
decisions.

Did you know that the overall rate of technological progress doubles every ten years? In other
words, we won't just experience a hundred years
of progress during the twenty-first century; it will
be more like twenty thousand years of progress
squeezed into one person's lifetime!

Is it any wonder that our brains are frazzled? Whether you love or loathe technology, one thing is certain: Change is here to stay. And when the seas of change keep threatening to engulf our shores, don't we all need constants to hold on to that can keep us anchored?

Consider the many gifts of God that exist within the natural world, and cling to the unchangeable and everlasting Father of heavenly lights, who created them all for you to enjoy.

∿ Pause and Sift ∿

Get outside and take a bike ride or go for a walk. Let creation's timeless beauty inspire you and remind you of who your God is.

Lord, thank you that your Word promises that you never change, even in a world that feels ever changing. Help me to stay anchored to the truth of who you are and your unfailing love for me.

Make Yourself Vulnerable

I take pleasure in my weaknesses....
For when I am weak, then I am strong.

2 CORINTHIANS 12:10

Boasting about my weaknesses has always seemed counterintuitive to me. And I don't find it easy to do.

But I'm slowly learning to stop juggling and stage-managing my life, because it's not about my lack of ability but rather the expanse of his. I'm discovering the truth of today's verse: There really is strength in weakness because it allows more of God's grace to rest on our lives.

When we share our struggles, others can come alongside to help; when we're brave enough to share the messy and vulnerable parts of our story, we can speak healing into someone else's life too.

God isn't looking for spiritual superheroes to advance his Kingdom. The Bible reminds me that he often chooses the least, the smallest, and the most unlikely things through which to demonstrate his power.

A shepherd boy overcomes a giant. Three hundred men crush an army of 120,000. Five loaves and two fish feed a hungry crowd. And the Savior of the world comes to Earth as a human baby. Don't you think that God might be able to use our smallness and our inadequacies too?

Don't settle for living your life as a performance before others; choose honesty, vulnerability, and a willingness to lean into weaknesses. Then watch God turn them into strengths.

∾ Pause and Sift ∾

Choose to be vulnerable this week. Reveal an area of weakness to a trusted friend or family member. As you share your struggles, ask for practical help or invite that person to pray for you.

Lord, help me to be quicker at
accepting my weaknesses, at choosing
vulnerability, and at leaning into your grace
so that your power may rest on me.

Live with Clarity

Be careful how you live. Don't live like fools, but
like those who are wise. Make the most of every
opportunity in these evil days. Don't act thoughtlessly,
but understand what the Lord wants you to do.

EPHESIANS 5:15-17

Every generation has its own cultural and spiritual blind spots. Busyness might be one of ours.

We constantly run from one thing to the next, trying to keep up with everyone and everything. We're overworked, overextended, and overstressed—but spiritually undernourished.

Deep down I think we know that this busyness isn't really making us more productive or creative or really helping us enjoy better lives. But too often we get caught up in it just the same.

Busyness is a spiritual problem because it prevents us from properly connecting with God, with others he has placed in our lives, and even with our own hearts.

When we're too busy, we often forget to pray and invite God into the moments of our day. We also tend to just skim the social surface and go through the motions of conversation with others, failing to really listen. We stop making space for self-reflection, for processing our emotions, and for becoming a healthier version of ourselves.

Maybe that's why Paul cautions us in today's verses to be careful how we live. Let's approach each day wisely in these busy times, making the most of every opportunity by taking the time to really understand what God is asking us to do.

∽ Pause and Sift ∽

Do you know what God wants you to prioritize right now? If you're not sure, ask him for clarity, and then streamline and simplify.

Lord, I want to live wisely in this rushed and hurried world. Show me where I might need to reorder and reprioritize so I can gain greater clarity.

Some Things
Take Time

I am certain that God, who began the good work within you, will continue his work until it is finally finished on the day when Christ Jesus returns.

PHILIPPIANS 1:6

We live in an age of impatience, when we're so used to having instant access to all the information and services and entertainment that we could want. No wonder God's sense of timing can feel so frustratingly slow to us!

But doing everything at an ever-faster and more efficient pace is not actually a biblical value.

Whenever I think about the unfolding story of Creation and redemption, I see a God who is simply not in a hurry—a God who is not influenced or bound by human time at all.

And whenever I read about the biblical heroes of faith, I see men and women whose encounters with God required great patience and perseverance. Waiting on God's timing had to be exasperating for some, but he is always committed to doing all things well.

The truth is that God is not sluggish or dawdling. He is patient, thorough, and unpressured by time, so he can teach us that truly important things like maturity and character don't happen overnight.

It's so easy to get wound up, frustrated, or disillusioned when God's timing doesn't match our agenda. But since he isn't in a hurry, we don't have to be either. We simply need to trust in his timing and submit to his ways.

∾ Pause and Sift ∾

Ask God to show you one small, practical change you can make this week that will help you live a slower, simpler, and more soulful life.

Lord, help me to trust in your timing, remembering that you value depth over surface change, steadiness over hurriedness, and thoroughness over haste.

Chase Your Dreams

Do not despise these small beginnings,
for the LORD rejoices to see the work begin.

ZECHARIAH 4:10

Have you ever dreamed of doing something different with your life but for some reason held back? Perhaps you decided it was going to cost too much or take up too much time, or maybe you just weren't sure where to begin.

It's never hard to find excuses for why something shouldn't be started or can't be done. But what a shame when we talk ourselves out of taking a risk or trying something new before we've even begun.

For the longest time I didn't pursue my dream of writing, even though lots of people encouraged me to. I was worried that I wasn't good enough and didn't have anything interesting to say. But how would I know if I didn't even try?

You can't keep putting things off or saying, "Maybe one day," because days turn into years.

So I began journaling my thoughts, blogging

short essays, and getting articles published. Most of it was pretty average. But I didn't need to begin with perfection. I just needed to begin.

If you have a dream in your heart, don't wait for that mythical moment when the conditions are just right or when you have enough time.

Start small, start simple . . . , and accept that you won't be perfect right away; good enough is good enough. God doesn't despise small beginnings, and neither should we.

∾ Pause and Sift ∾

Do you have a "one day" dream? Begin to identify some small steps you can take this week to move the dream a little closer to reality.

Lord, I'm sorry for letting my own
sense of smallness hold me back. Help me
to step out in confidence, knowing that
you delight in my small beginnings.

Notes

PRACTICE SELF-CARE

"Incredibly, there's an $11 billion self-care industry in the United States today . . ." See
Charlotte Lieberman, "How Self-Care Became So Much Work," *Harvard Business Review*, August 10, 2018, https://hbr.org/2018/08/how-self-care-became-so-much-work.

USE THE DELAYS

"Google has found that 53 percent of us will abandon a mobile web page if it takes
longer than three seconds to load." Jay Castro, "Increase the speed of your mobile
site with this toolkit," Google Ad Manager, October 13, 2016, https://www.blog
.google/products/admanager/increase-speed-of-your-mobile-site-wi.

TURN DOWN THE NOISE

"Are you on Facebook? Each day more than 300 million photos get uploaded, and each
minute 510,000 comments are posted and 293,000 statuses are updated." See
Bernard Marr, "How Much Data Do We Create Every Day? The Mind-Blowing
Stats Everyone Should Read," *Forbes*, May 21, 2018, https://www.forbes.com/sites
/bernardmarr/2018/05/21/how-much-data-do-we-create-every-day-the-mind
-blowing-stats-everyone-should-read/#38bdac0660ba.

"Do you use Twitter? An incredible 500 million new tweets are posted every single day!"
See Kit Smith, "126 Amazing Social Media Statistics and Facts," Brandwatch,
December 30, 2019, https://www.brandwatch.com/blog/amazing-social-media
-statistics-and-facts/.

LEARN TO BREATHE

"The average adult takes between 17,280 and 23,040 breaths every day." See Ann
Brown, "How Many Breaths Do You Take Each Day?" *The EPA Blog*, April 28,
2014, https://blog.epa.gov/2014/04/28/how-many-breaths-do-you-take-each-day/.

LESS IS MORE

"He goes on to say that we are the branches his Father is pruning, and when we produce
much fruit, we are Jesus' true disciples." See John 15:2, 5, 8.

DEAL WITH DOUBT

"My God, my God, why have you abandoned me?" Mark 15:34.

SLEEP WELL

"In one study, more than half of the US adults surveyed said they struggled to get a good night's sleep at least once a week." "Why Americans Can't Sleep," *Consumer Reports*, January 14, 2016, https://www.consumerreports.org/sleep/why-americans -cant-sleep/.

"Psychophysiological issues such as stress, anxiety, and the inability to switch off from the day are said to cause around 70 percent of these sleep problems." "Causes of Poor Sleep," *Sleeprate Blog*, October 15, 2018, https://www.sleeprate.com/causes -poor-sleep/.

FIND YOUR CREW

"In fact, almost half of those who responded to a 2018 online survey reported regularly feeling alone." See "Over Half of Americans Report Feeling Like No One Knows Them Well," Ipsos, May 1, 2018, https://www.ipsos.com/en-us/news-polls/us -loneliness-index-report.

TRY LAUGHING

"Did you know that laughing is scientifically proven to reduce feelings of stress and improve our mood? What's more, it can actually increase our ability to cope with physical pain and illness and increase our immunity." See Mayo Clinic staff, "Stress relief from laughter? It's no joke," Mayo Clinic, April 5, 2019, https://www.mayoclinic.org/healthy-lifestyle/stress-management/in-depth/stress -relief/art-20044456.

"In fact, tests have shown that watching just fifteen minutes of comedy can make us 10 percent more resistant to pain." Jennifer Welsh, "Why Laughter May Be the Best Pain Medicine," *Scientific American*, September 14, 2011, https://www .scientificamerican.com/article/why-laughter-may-be-the-best-pain-medicine/.

EMBRACE THE JOURNEY

"If everything had gone as planned, the trip from Mount Sinai to the Promised Land should have only taken them eleven days." See Deuteronomy 1:2.

FIGHT DECISION FATIGUE

"In 1976 there were just nine thousand different products in the average store, but less than twenty years later, there were already about thirty thousand." See Steven Waldman, "The Tyranny of Choice," in *Consumer Society in American History: A Reader*, ed. Lawrence B. Glickman (Ithaca, New York: Cornell University Press, 1999), 360 (chapter taken from *New Republic*, January 27, 1992).

BE SMART WITH YOUR PHONE

"According to some studies, the average American checks their mobile phone eighty times a day and spends around three hours browsing its small screen." See

SWNS, "Americans Check Their Phones 80 Times a Day: Study," *New York Post*, November 8, 2017, https://nypost.com/2017/11/08/americans-check-their -phones-80-times-a-day-study/ and Yoram Wurmser, "US Time Spent with Mobile 2019," eMarketer, May 30, 2019, https://www.emarketer.com/content/us-time -spent-with-mobile-2019.

STOP THE HUSTLE

"You are worried and upset about many things, but few things are needed—or indeed only one." Luke 10:41-42, niv.

ALWAYS AWARE

"Surely the Lord is in this place, and I wasn't even aware of it." Genesis 28:16.

RELEASE YOUR WORRY

"In fact, anxiety disorders affect about one in five adults in America today." See "Facts & Statistics," Anxiety and Depression Association of America, accessed January 24, 2020, https://adaa.org/about-adaa/press-room/facts-statistics.

GET BACK UP

"A common motto in Silicon Valley, where nine out of ten new tech start-ups fail, is 'fail fast, fail often.'" Rory Carroll, "Silicon Valley's Culture of Failure . . . and 'The Walking Dead' It Leaves Behind," *Guardian* (Manchester), June 28, 2014, https://www.theguardian.com/technology/2014/jun/28/silicon-valley-startup -failure-culture-success-myth.

"Did you know that James Dyson went through 5,127 prototypes before he successfully launched the world's first bagless vacuum cleaner?" See "Our Story: The Accidental Engineer," The James Dyson Foundation, accessed April 1, 2020, https://www .jamesdysonfoundation.com/who-we-are/our-story.html.

"Or that Henry Ford closed two failed car companies before launching the world's first mass-produced car?" See History.com editors, "This Day in History—August 15: Henry Ford Leaves Edison to Start Automobile Company," History, last updated August 14, 2019, https://www.history.com/this-day-in-history/henry-ford-leaves -edison-to-start-automobile-company.

LOVE YOURSELF

"A recent global study by Dove, a manufacturer of beauty products, surveyed women from thirteen developed countries and found that the majority surveyed were self-conscious about their appearance. Many respondents admitted they opted out of important life events because they didn't like the way they looked." See "New Dove Research Finds Beauty Pressures Up, and Women and Girls Calling for Change," Cision PR Newswire, June 21, 2016, https://www.prnewswire.com/news-releases /new-dove-research-finds-beauty-pressures-up-and-women-and-girls-calling-for -change-583743391.html.

NOTICE THE GOOD

"Did you know there are 9,096 stars in the night sky visible from the earth?" See Bob King, "9,096 Stars in the Sky—Is That All?" *Sky & Telescope*, September 17, 2014, https://skyandtelescope.org/astronomy-resources/how-many-stars-night-sky-09172014/.

"In fact, before this verse, the phrase 'it was good' is repeated six times." See Genesis 1:3, 10, 12, 18, 21, 25, NKJV.

"The average person in the United States spends 93 percent of their time enclosed in either buildings or vehicles." See Neil E Klepeis et al., "The National Human Activity Pattern Survey (NHAPS): A Resource for Assessing Exposure to Environmental Pollutants," *Journal of Exposure Science and Environmental Epidemiology*, no. 11 (July 2001): 231–52, https://doi.org/10.1038/sj.jea.7500165.

CUT THE COMPLAINING

Facts cited in this article are taken from Travis Bradberry, "How Complaining Rewires Your Brain for Negativity," Talentsmart, accessed January 27, 2020, https://www.talentsmart.com/articles/How-Complaining-Rewires-Your-Brain-for-Negativity-2147446676-p-1.html.

LEARN TO LINGER

"Jesus took time to linger and converse with a Samaritan woman at a well; time to befriend and eat with corrupt tax collectors; time to listen to and answer the questions of a rich young ruler; and time to stop and heal a blind beggar on the roadside, as today's passage describes." See John 4:1-26, Matthew 9:10-11, and Mark 10:17-27, 46-52.

OVERCOME SELF-DOUBT

"One major corporation found that men felt confident applying for a job when they met 60 percent of the criteria, whereas most women applied only if they felt they met 100 percent of the requirements." See Tara Sophia Moore, "Why Women Don't Apply for Jobs Unless They're 100% Qualified," *Harvard Business Review*, August 25, 2014, https://hbr.org/2014/08/why-women-dont-apply-for-jobs-unless-theyre-100-qualified.

PAY MORE ATTENTION

"The truth is that chasing after our own glory and fame is the original sin that caused Satan to fall from heaven; he wanted to become more, to become his own god." See Ezekiel 28:17-18.

WHEN THE UNEXPECTED HAPPENS

"The Bible actually warns us to be ready for all kinds of trials and challenges in life. And why do we allow them to unsettle us so easily when the Bible encourages us to see our difficulties as opportunities for growth?" See 1 Peter 4:12, John 16:33, and James 1:2-4.

WHEN IS IT ENOUGH?

"Marketing experts estimate that we've gone from being exposed to about five hundred advertisements and marketing messages a day back in the 1970s to consuming around five thousand in 2006." See Caitlyn Johnson, "Cutting through Advertising Clutter," Sunday Morning, September 17, 2006, https://www.cbsnews.com/news/cutting-through-advertising-clutter/.

"Is anything worth more than your soul?" Matthew 16:26.

HUMOROUS RELIEF

"I've heard it said that 10 percent of life is about what happens to you, and 90 percent is about how you respond." Attributed to Charles Swindoll.

"Did you know that when you laugh, it actually causes physical changes to your body that reduce anxiety and stress and boost your overall sense of well-being?" See Mayo Clinic Staff, "Stress Relief from Laughter? It's No Joke," April 5, 2019, https://www.mayoclinic.org/healthy-lifestyle/stress-management/in-depth/stress-relief/art-20044456.

CALM IN A CRISIS

"Teacher, don't you care that we're going to drown?" Mark 4:38.

KEEP IT SIMPLE

"no other commandment is greater than *these*." Emphasis added.

"God is love." 1 John 4:8.

ACTIVATE YOURSELF

"In fact, research indicates that just twenty minutes of physical activity a day can significantly improve your emotional and physical well-being." See "How Exercise Makes You Happy," Australian Fitness Academy, March 7, 2018, https://www.fitnesseducation.edu.au/blog/health/how-exercise-makes-you-happy/.

EXPERIENCE HIS COMFORT

"the God of all comfort." 2 Corinthians 1:3, NIV.

CHANGE IS HERE TO STAY

"Did you know that the overall rate of technological progress doubles every ten years? In other words, we won't just experience a hundred years of progress during the twenty-first century; it will be more like twenty thousand years of progress squeezed into one person's lifetime!" See Ray Kurzweil, "The Law of Accelerating Returns," Kurzweil: Accelerating Intelligence, March 7, 2001, https://www.kurzweilai.net/the-law-of-accelerating-returns.

MAKE YOURSELF VULNERABLE

"A shepherd boy overcomes a giant. Three hundred men crush an army of 120,000. Five loaves and two fish feed a hungry crowd. And the Savior of the world comes to Earth as a human baby." See 1 Samuel 17; Judges 8:4, 10-12; Matthew 14:13-21; and Luke 2.

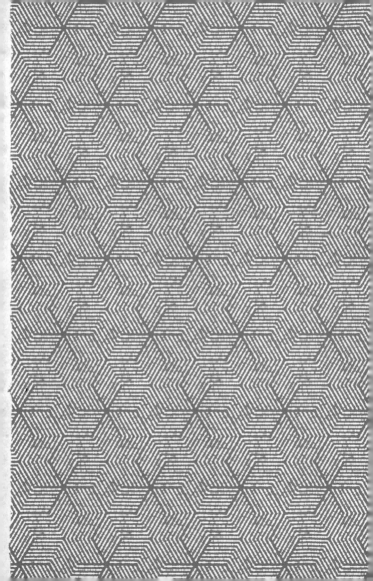

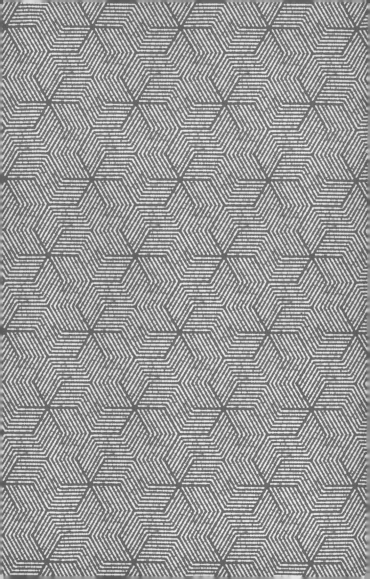